A Note Sent to the Author:

"I love this kind of book combining chronicle, personal history and fiction. The portrait of the father ... is the most moving thing I have read lately. Bravo! How fortunate to meet Leonard Gardner, the author of that marvel that is Fat City, *to listen to jazz in the old Blackhawk of San Francisco, places that I dreamed of in my younger days. The anecdote of the heroin addict who interrupts the young protagonist while he's with his* doña *is a beautiful turn—not at all sordid—in a book that has so much to do with tenderness and innocence."* **Edgardo Rodríguez Juliá**, Puerto Rican novelist and chronicler, author of *The Renunciation*, *Cortijo's Wake*, and other books awaiting publication in English (from an email, 6 de Oct. 2020).

Two Ways West

(Exodus)

Two Ways West (Exodus)

Marc Zimmerman

Library of Congress Control Number (LCC): 2024911239

Listed in the Catalogue of the Library of Congress: 1. Fiction 2. Autofiction 3. Jewish American literature. 4. U.S. ethnic literature 5. coming of age 6. U.S. 1950s university life 7. U.S. East Coast-West Coast
LACASA Chicago Books
2120 W. Concord Place
Chicago, IL 60647
mzimmerman1939@gmail.com
Tel. 281-513-9475.
Website: www.marczimmerman.net

Horace Greeley:
"Go West, young man!"

Cormac McCarthy
(giving Yeats a U.S. twist):
"[It's] no country for old men."

Dedication

My Father, Mother, Sister, Brother-in-law
and cousin, Carol Zimmerman, RIP
To My Nieces and Great-Niece
To my son Carlos and his Family
And of course, to my incredible wife Esther
And all our family members.

CONTENTS

Book One.

One Way to California

(The Father)

1. Invocation

Let me tell you about my father— or at least how it was that he, and of course my mother, moved from New Jersey to California.

First you should know that they got there in a deluxe 57 Cadillac, long and black, with those arched and flashing fins gliding out on a road straight to heaven. Power steering, power brakes, electric windows, remote control aerial, AM/FM, stereo speakers, AC—the works, as they'd say in those days. The works, except for its not having a couple of gizmos that would have made it perfect. But it was after all a pretty deluxe showboat of a car that he took or, rather, that took his wife and him all the way to the West Coast. And I've already kind of half-told you more than one reason why he went.

My father always thought big, dreamed big. His big thinking led him to over-stock his over-big, debt-ridden restaurant, only half of which was his, and caused him to travel with the Big Men—which meant big gin rummy games, big bookie tabs and therefore big payoffs of big money, less than half of which was his. The rest of the cash he took on the sly from the till, or, what soon proved easier, from banks. Since the one he "borrowed" from was his own brother, he didn't go to jail.

My mother could never figure out, and my father never told her, exactly what the money was for, or why so many banks in Jersey always gave him credit on the business, even without his brother's signature and even after they were told to desist from so doing. But the bad debts, for all their mystery, had to be paid. And that was my mother's job. That is, she worked, hovering over the grey metal cash register, keeping my father's hands out as best she could, while the wives and mistresses of the *really* Big Men dangled their feet over the sides of Miami Beach swimming pools.

Finally, though, after years of evasions, the debts caught up with my father. My uncle had torn at his hair for years; his wife pointed to the peeling plaster of their ceiling, the belittled opportunities for their children; and now, most of his hair gone and the rest graying rapidly, his wife embittered, and his big brother's big image shattered forever, my uncle said, more as an epitaph than as an ultimatum, it's either you or me, Sam.

This story has to do with my father's reaction to his brother's words, with what he did, with what happened to him. So I guess I should be more careful in telling you what led to that reaction. But I have to warn you, that I can only imagine what he thought and how he felt. Because he never told me any of this, hardly a word. Some of it I know from what my sister said, or what my mother said, in one unguarded moment or another over many years. But he never told me much of it, hardly anything. He would die without telling me his version of things, and I only tried to piece together what happened as best I could.

Of course, the story, told this way, may well be untrue—at least in one way or another. But that's probably the case of most stories, and the story may be worth telling anyway.

2. Some Things to Know

There are some things you should know. At age 50, my father was a 320-pound glandular mess. He was bald with a nose that projected beyond his puffed cheeks like the hooked beak of a stuffed and stymied bird. His eyes were were half-hidden by heavy, half-closed lids. The flaccid, yellowing jowls, the cynically humorous curve to his thick lips made—all this made his face a mask.

His body was gutted by infirmities of all kinds. A calcium deficiency blotched his hands brown; warts rose like barnacles on his neck and trunk. He had sciatica, a bad back, some inexplicable illness that shot up from spine or spleen and skewed his left eye; he had diabetes, an ulcer and worst of all, kidneys that produced crystals and stopped and tore at his urinary track about twice a year, assaulting and racking his body, and (what finally did him in) taking its toll on his initially strong and intractable heart. All his diseases cut into the things he could eat, and all his disease-geared diets clashed. This was the price he paid, the product of a process—all for being who and what he was and what being all that made him want to be or do. In the end, aging, wilting and heading toward death in the California sun, he would not feel so big. Ills and pills would not leave him so big either.

But before, in his Jersey salad days, he'd gone about his business like two workaholics and two hedonists trapped in the same body. It must've seemed to him like all his Jewish buddies had made it big during the war, even as the oh-so-chosen people were being hounded and murdered in Europe. In the 1950s, he found himself playing that desperate game of catch-up where you only see the ones who are ahead, and where they've already got such a leg up on you that they only moved further into the lead the harder you ran. Life meant work, work meant success, success meant consuming, consuming meant achievement—and even fun. So he worked sixteen hours a day and then danced Latin music like a bloated Astaire and then played cards (disastrously) much of the night.

The only way I can account for all that raw energy is by thinking of the way he must have seen those around him and then, after all was said and done, by chalking it up to stubbornness and will. Enough of both he had for certain. Where he got them Yahweh only knows, but they were deeper and greater than I have seen in any other man. Deeper and greater and maybe more wasted.

There was that night at Roosevelt Raceway, when he'd gone to the bathroom three breaks running. At first I thought nothing of it. We were supposed to be partners betting out of a joint pool. But he always wandered off, and never really tried to hide the fact that he was placing some pretty hefty side-bets of his own. (He only let me know directly when he won and wanted to cover some losses of our dipping pool funds.) But after the second john break, I began to feel his tension—I saw that hardening at his mouth corners: one of the few facial expressions he could muster. After the fourth race, I saw him grit his teeth and press his lips together. He sweated and squinted, his eyes watered. Dad, I said, let's get out of here. But he wouldn't go, he had Big Money on the fifth race, and he was going to stick it out, even though we both knew by now what was coming.

Well, he lost the fifth, but won the sixth and only let me get him to the car after he'd stood in line to collect his winnings. All the way home from Long Island, I heard his sighs, his choked gasps and groans, as he spasmed and flailed in the back seat.

I had to ward off his arm flings, his fists pounding on windows and cushions. I crimped my neck and clutched the wheel, tearing down the long highway, across Manhattan to the Tunnel, and then along the Turnpike, and home. Finally we made it to the apartment complex parking lot. I jostled and pried him, a wobbling, unmanageable dead-weight mass, out of the car and up the walk; I stuffed him through the door and into the house, cleared off his blankets and prepared to push him onto his bed. But before he went down, he gave me a smile out from below some six levels of pain and misery and handed me a bloody kidney stone the size of a marble.

Such was his stubbornness, his will, his pride, his way. This is what he brought to the big race that was his life.

3. The Will, Money and Friday Night Flights

I suppose that when it's important for you to think people think you're important or special, then you've got to be or do or get what it is that would make you feel you've created the needed illusion. If you'd met my father, you'd have been repelled or embarrassed at first; but the feeling wouldn't have lasted for long. At the deep center of his bloated mass his will sent out yeah-saying signals, life-affirming bleeps in the fog. So he came to have his famous assets: his extravagant generosity ("always tip big, son, never let them think you're cheap"), and while we saw little of them at home, where his "little problem" made everything he said and did sputter and die like so many wet firecrackers, a great sense of compassion and humility (he had plenty of both), and a notoriously "fabulous" sense of humor (this joined with a memory for jokes and a knack for telling them)—all in all, the neat package of traits which added up to be what they used to call "a real mensch."

The fact is, my father had all the assets but one. My father lived in America the Beautiful, but he didn't have money.

It's hard to write about money especially if you're trying to deal with your father, and when you're not really sure what your writing could mean as you try to imagine what your father thought and wanted, without really knowing if that's the way it was. I have trouble accepting the fact that this man who left me so troubled, had unknowingly bartered his every smile or tear, every lift of eye or finger, every damned flick of cigar ash, to win the people and do the things he thought he had to do, to bring him the stash of cash that was to ever elude him anyway.

His own mother had preserved the gentility she had nurtured as a seamstress (or tailor's aid) in the Tsar's court; but his father had maintained the brutal ways he'd learned as commissary provisioner in the Tsar's army. He was one of those Jews who made himself valuable to his bosses—in his case by entering peasant villages ahead of the troops to terrorize the peasants into offering up their wines and meats, their cheeses and chickens, and maybe their daughters too. He must have felt betrayed by the pogroms, and he took his wife and infant child (my father) and came to the U.S., bypassing the New York City Jewish ghetto as fast as he could, taking whatever route available in those days to get to New Jersey and enter the U.S.A. for real.

But how could the man ever expect to fit in the community where he lived? What kind of Jews were these who hardly spoke a word of Yiddish? What kind of Jew was that, so crude and foul-tongued and hard-drinking? Whoever heard of a Jewish drunk? Unable to hold a job, he drifted from business to business, never getting anywhere. He abused his wife, his oldest son and then others of his growing brood. My father dropped out of school early to support his mother, his brothers and his sister. The aging patriarch became a pariah in the community; he drifted in and out of the house, gone for days at a time, turning harsher and more bitter with each passing month. Perhaps a killer of peasants in the Old World, he became known to curse his own people and wish them dead when he had a few drinks. He grew to hate everyone, above all himself. One cold morning in 1936, the Great Depression and he too now in the deepest funk over some kind of financial transaction with a family member, he stuck his head in the gas oven and killed himself. However loveless and harsh their marriage, his long-suffering wife, my father's mother, (maybe out of despair, maybe out of joy, who knows?) collapsed and died the very next day.

I was born only three years later, my life perhaps an answer to their death. But my father never once talked about them, never once brought them up, skirted the subject if I or someone else mentioned them. At least outwardly, he had so cut off himself from the mainsprings of his life, that I have only been able to piece them together after who knows how many years of living and asking. This story is another stage of the piecing together, the work of someone still trying to understand his father's past, to make sense of his own past and future, and whatever meaning they might be said to have on this planet.

Can we see it all in a nutshell—or through a glass ever so darkly? Born of a family alienated from its own community, my father sought to become a community pillar. Given the fact that he never became rich, he did pretty damn well. He was a founder and first president of his synagogue, became a 32nd degree Mason, a Shriner and who knows what else. But he started with problems and he never could overcome them. The eldest son, he had borne the brunt of his father's failures and violence, and long before he'd accepted full responsibility for his brothers and sister, carrying them on his shoulders, dropping out of the seventh grade, selling newspapers and then working in the deli-business, helping each one of his siblings to get started in his kind of work. He was still helping them, struggling out of the muck, when the depression hit another big snag and pushed him so far down, he couldn't fully get up even with the war.

Then, as what was happening happened in the old world, many of the new world Jews amassed their stakes, and, by hook and at least a fair number by crook, catapulted themselves into the established and ever-upward bound middle class and even beyond. All around him, friends and relatives were making it—and there was even the case of his Communist butcher (and concert singer) cousin, who tried desperately to hold onto his politics even after he had made a million because of special wartime meat deals his wife handled while, as a CP-United Front enlistee private, he peeled potatoes in a local camp waiting for a chance to fight the Nazis that never came.

Coming out of the war, realizing how much his wife had made, he tried to give the bulk of his money to help rebuild the Soviet Union. His wife didn't quite agree, keeping control over the money, and showing how commitment and loyalty to her adopted country led a good, upstanding Jewish woman like herself to oppose her husband's crazy ideas, buy a lifetime Jewish country club membership, and send their son and daughter to the best private schools and universities money could help buy.

Meanwhile her husband, confused by his new wealth, his fancy new home and well-educated children he increasingly couldn't understand, spent his dwindling days listening to the classical music albums he so loved, inviting over my father and other cousins (my uncles, but not the brother my father would sometimes have to rob—that one had to stay at the restaurant) so they could play gin rummy while I sat in the next room, hearing those great classical albums, those great Italian singers and conductors, and yes, those sublime and vulgar Wagnerian swoops and swoons of Furtwängler conducting Kirsten Flagstad.

I remember one uncle—best known for his Nat King Cole imitations—shouting, how can you let the boy listen to those Nazis? But there I sat drenched in great music, oblivious to ideologies, while the men slammed down their cards and I dreamed of another world, another life—until 10 p.m. came and my card-playing elder kin and I came together for the Friday night Gillette Blue Blade boxing matches, a time for the Brown Bomber, for Sugar Ray Robinson, Rocky Graziano, Jake Lamotta, Willie Pep, Sandy Sadler, Kid Gavilán (what a bolo punch) and all the rest—but with not one new Jew in the whole bunch.

In the war's aftermath, now in his forties, my father made the desperate plunge to break out of oblivion, to catch up with friends and relatives and taste the fruits of cash and success. Many of those friends and relatives had begun moving out of the neighborhood when he couldn't and didn't; their kids started going to Ivy League schools, while his own daughter had to spell her mother at the cash register and go to a third rate college, until she dropped out, got married and moved to California to escape it all. And meanwhile his one and only beloved boychik got turned down by all the rich girls who no longer lived in the neighborhood, and had to ride his rocking horse to pick trotters and pacers to fund one, but only one, year at a second level Ivy League college before we all followed my sister into a California exile, where, realizing there was no money and also that my beloved father was either a smalltime crook or at least a reckless gamer intent on ruining us all, I ended up going down the social ladder and attending a commuter state u. while I took on one part-time job after another until I had to draft this story one fine though not so happy day.

I don't doubt for a minute that my father justified all his mad, mindless maneuvers to avoid exactly what happened to my sister and me. But starting late and without all the advantages, my father only went so far; and by the definitions he accepted, failed. Failing, he had to give the appearance of success, find ways to get to Miami and (the best) Havana, buy his wife a mink—get all the outward signs of something that wasn't. So it was that he got involved with bankers, loan sharks, bookies and other assorted Mafia small fry. So it was that somewhere between his good intentions and his actions, money had stuck up its giant head. He'd become caught up in it—its ups and downs, its actions and transactions. So what came to be the story of my father was the story of money—the ways he tried to get it and spend it, and the ways it got and spent him and us.

4. Being Big, Settling In

My father had to be big, a big giver, a big tipper—always with a wad in his pocket, a cigar in his mouth, even if he choked on it. He had to go to the "classy" places and pick up the tab. Working long hours every day, mixing with men who paraded their new wealth, he nurtured desperate dreams of sudden wealth, of heaps of money that would end his miserable and shameful obscurity. In other men, he was sharp enough to detect this madness and scorn it. In himself, he denied its existence and yet it lived. But in some funny, frustrating way: he could not smash his fetters completely, and so he never robbed a bank or stormed the mint. Instead, he cheated his brother and wife.

The first time he took money, it must have hurt him. But the very fact that he was a "feeling man" made it impossible for him to live with a burden of guilt. Basically he wanted to continue living as he felt compelled to and still maintain a good opinion of himself. So, when he took the money he must've said, this is the one and only time. And since he had lived through the first family betrayal, the second had to be a little easier. Of course, he was a man who dreaded condemnation far more than he dreaded stealing. And when, after a while, the confrontations became insufferable, he became a man avoiding the future, disappointed looks and scandalized accusations. For years, he played a cat-and-mouse game of paying off old debts by contracting new, of staving off my mother's discoveries by means of constant concealment and lies—all fronted by a bravura show that was designed to be "winning."

By the time his oldest debts were uncovered, it was easy not to feel guilty—they were so much part of a distanced past. Besides, a man gets tired of recriminations and regret; and if he finds a need to continue with their causes, he'll invent deceits to shield himself. If my father had been unable to believe his own lies and rationalizations, he would have been unable to carry the burden.

Over the years, he began to see his good opinion reflected by those around him—his big friends, and some of the lesser lights who frequented his restaurant. He was the grand host, the big sport, the swell guy. He had gradually sacrificed the respect of those closest to him. And when he could no longer see admiration written on their faces, he no longer relied on them to keep himself afloat.

There are some funny things involved here. By definition, my father had to be a "fine family man," one who thrived on intimacy, the home as refuge and the rest of it. He was a bright man, one who could be sensitive to others. He secretly prided himself on his ability not only with words but with paint, music, plants and just about everything. He was after all an artist of roasts and coleslaw and *hors d'oeuvres* trays—a master caterer like a master of theater. But he had long learned to regard his family and artistic sides as just trimmings, to be put aside with a sadness what was at least somewhat feigned. And so, despite the phoniness that was part of the package he had bought, you couldn't help but feel that he was one of those who were trapped into performing a role they were never meant to play.

I mean when you think about everything that went into his performances, and if you can somehow separate what his questionable acts (and you can't do it, I know) from the ends he hoped they would serve—when you think how he had succumbed to things, when you realize he didn't have any one he could level with for fear of exposure—then you realize how some of his best values and qualities had become terribly twisted and had turned against him. None of this is to excuse him. No, in the midst of all the circumstances and determinants, he had chosen. Somehow all his best impulses had become warped and had bred serpents. By an act of love—for his family, for his community, for himself—he had early fitted himself into a life he could never long conform to, and, never completely break with. Like other American Jews of his time and situation, he was on the road to "settling in" as best as he could—and if he couldn't do it by hook, he'd do it by crook.

5. A Complex Man, A Complex Reaction

So when my uncle finally held his breath and said what he had had to say for years on end, my father's reaction had to have been worthy of the complex man that he was. Don't get the idea that he was completely callous. No doubt he regretted all the sorrow he had caused, the bills that could only be met through the sacrifice of someone else. The nine years of work that had been reduced to pathetic absurdity because of his "little weakness." Perhaps he realized that his brother had had to play the failure to his own wife and kids to cover for what my father was doing. Surely he regretted that my mother viewed him with contempt, that because of his actions, she'd been forced to take control of all his affairs, making him accountable to her even for his cigar money.

But how much regretting can a man do? My father was a complex man, and he could go beyond callousness. He could say that whatever he'd done, he done it hoping his family would benefit. He could justify himself for the sake of his son's future. He could blame business problems on his brother's and wife's imagination not matching his own. In business and marriage, he could argue, that he had heavy, unwieldy weights around his neck. Wasn't he smarter than both of them, and hadn't he worked hard for years and years only to have to it all brought to naught through their constant interference? If he hadn't had the guts and know-how to win himself friends—big, substantial men according to anyone's standards—wouldn't his only leisure hours have been dominated by his wife's canasta clique or his brother's petty-anti, penny-a-point card playing friends—small timers all?

He could point to the dreams he'd had as a boy—dreams that had been thwarted because certainly his father wouldn't heed the hungry yelps of his brothers and sisters. Hadn't he earned a little slack for keeping his family alive, for helping his brothers get started, for being able to support their own families at all? Hadn't he sacrificed his own education, the very possibilities of his life? Was he meant to be no more than a food peddler? Didn't he have all kinds of potentials that out of love and duty he had been unable to develop? Hadn't every Lions Club in Union County gone out of their way to invite him as their after-dinner speaker? Hadn't his fellow religionists honored him for his service and sacrifice? All his lofty dreams he'd given up to peddle newspapers at 5 a.m. and in a deli until 10 p.m. And for what? For a brother with no sense of foresight, no sense of bigness and no ... no gratitude.

For having taught his brother everything he knew about the food business, having given much of his life to others, wasn't he not now entitled to some simple pleasures? Was his whole life to be one great sacrifice? Didn't he have any rights? Oh, it was true he hadn't counted on having to milk the business. How'd he know the bookies would be at his throat? He had to take the money—yes. But he swore to pay it back. Certainly he never thought he'd have to borrow again and again. But the debts were being paid, weren't they? And after all he'd done for his brother, so what if it hurt a little?

And as for my mother, well didn't he love her as a man should love his wife? And it wasn't that she was the most brilliant woman in the history of the world, either, nor the most beautiful, if you really wanted to know. Not that he didn't appreciate her, far be it from him not to. But hadn't she gotten ample reward by being able to lord it over him—being able to call the shots with someone for the first time in her life? And her always nagging him for being overweight. Sam, you're getting too fat. Sam, don't sit down and rip your pants. Sam, don't stick your hands in your pockets. As if his weight made any difference. As if eating wasn't after all an occupational hazard he had to live with. And, yes, maybe even a sign of affluence and ethnic pride. As if they held a monopoly on being right and good. As far as he could see, the whole thing was unfortunate, but it was obvious to anyone of insight who the real victim was.

Worse than callous, my father was foolish and self-deluded. His first resulting rationalization was a crude one: I'll leave my brother with this heart breaker of a business. He had certainly caused enough trouble, let's see if he can take it. Basically a generous man, however, he found no satisfaction in this formulation. And so he fashioned for himself a set of logical imperatives that enabled him to triumph. *Desperate smugness*: my brother is uncooperative; *disdain*: he's ungrateful; *self-pity*: I've always loved my brother; *triumphant*: I forgive my brother.

Thus it became an act of great magnanimity for him to hide his brother's baleful blame. Of course, knowing what he knew, he couldn't stay in the business. He forgave his brother, of course, but that didn't mean he had to continue taking unnecessary abuse. Better to leave while they were still on good terms. End in a businesslike, amicable manner. So he came to believe it was time to get out of an unfortunate trap. He convinced himself that he was tired of accusations and of work that was fruitless. He told himself—and then his friends—that when a man in his position, who had worked so hard and so long, was past the age of fifty, it was the moment to stop the merry-go-round, to get off and start relaxing and enjoying life while there was still time. No, he wasn't going to retire—my mother was quick to remind him that this was impossible—and he told his friends that of course a man like himself couldn't be completely inactive. He would move to a pleasant, warm climate, and work maybe a few hours a day and just—just take it easy.

6. Florida or California

And where was this retiring magnate going to settle? But there could be no question about it—at least not to my father. Where were most of his friends going to live? Where is a successful first generation American Jew (of good will) supposed to live?

But my mother didn't like the idea of Miami Beach. My father knew too many people there to gamble with and borrow from. Besides, she reminded him, you're going to have to work. And not just to fill his leisure hours either. Miami Beach wasn't the place for a man his age to get a job. Don't be silly, he said. And in his mind, you could see he expected a good two hundred thousand from the business. No (the dream blossomed), two hundred fifty, three hundred thousand. And he said it.

My mother had grown haggard from trying to understand him, from living day to day not knowing when he'd do some terrible thing next; she'd become bitter and sharp-tongued. You're crazy! Absolutely out of your head! We'll be lucky to get seventy-five thousand. Of course this was absurd. But he thought he'd try another tack—the martyr. Well, what do you want me to do? Tell me. I'll go to Scranton and work in a coal mine if that's what you want. No! She insisted. To California! To their daughter and grandchildren. At least there he stood half a chance to get a job; there they needed men who could cut a corned beef or make a potato salad that tasted just right; there she'd at least have her daughter who'd care about her, to say nothing about taking her side (for who thought anything about her here: *Sarah-the-hag, Sarah-the-drag, Sarah-the-nag, Sarah-now-Sam-this-or-that*) if he should wind up pulling his old stunts again.

They'd been to California on visits for recent summer vacations, even though it had meant not being able to afford winters with his friends in Miami. It wasn't that he didn't like the West Coast, mind you (could his daughter or his son-in-law make a bad move?). The future was in California, no doubt about it. But California was not his cup of tea. California was only second best.

A man in his position *had* to go to Miami. Why I don't think he knew precisely. Maybe he saw California as orange trees mowed over by asphalt and iron, as the speed and force of the future, young, hard and ruthless, and not the golf and sun of a leisure well-earned. Whatever the reason, he knew her estimate of their business share was way below the mark, so he told her they'd wait and decide after the selling terms were settled. And meanwhile he told his well-meaning friends he was Miami-bound.

7. The Settlement

It was my father's estimate that proved absurd as he found out on a day in early March when he walked with confidence and indeed a kind of benign arrogance into the accountant's office and just minutes later walked out, his future place in life all but determined.

The substance of the meeting went something like this. The accountant figured the business was worth $365,000. My father groaned: the business was worth way over half a million, and the accountant was in it with his brother or someone to rob him of his due. But what you don't seem to understand, Sam, is that the business owes. Well sure it owes, but—... It owes about 150 grand—including a good chunk to banks for various unaccountable transactions, the accountant added, fairly glaring, and then turning away, taking off his horn rims and wiping them with a piece of torn tissue.

My father grumbled but held his peace; he grumbled once more and more deeply when he found his share set at $130,000. Politely, the accountant hid certain miscellaneous embezzlements behind a mendacious statement claiming that my uncle's initial investment exceeded my father's by so many thousands. Thus, history received the kind of sugarcoating we've since learned to associate with the crimes of Stalin.

Of course, my father had his own version of the story. He was appalled at the colossal ingratitude. In his heart he thought he'd been swindled. But he was a big man. And though he saw his life getting a jolt (if not the shaft) and though the prospect of some grim future days began to loom before him, he made no scene. In effect, it was not his style; it did not become a big man to whine or wheedle or wheeze, and so... he said nothing. He said nothing and did nothing, even when they worked out terms that were far from inspiring. First, they were to receive $10,000 in cash. The rest was to be paid off in monthly installments of $1,000 over the next ten years while they sought to establish themselves in their new life. He knew all too well it was peanuts, a deal geared strictly to the tax structure and with no interest addon. But he knew that because of his finagling, the business could afford no other arrangement. All the years, all the work and just twelve thousand coming in each year so my uncle and his family could begin to live a life. The whole thing was chicken shit, and he knew it. But still he said nothing, did nothing. And then again, what was there to say or do? You see, I think there was more to my father's silence than his being above it all. I think that for all his swagger and ability to fool himself, he'd had some inkling into the outcome of this meeting. I mean $250, 300 thousand had been another one of his desperate dreams of sudden heaps of money. He'd tried to make himself believe his estimate by recklessly boasting of his semiretirement in Miami. Perhaps he'd hoped he could will it into reality. But he'd never completely believed it. And when he was confronted ever so gently, all he could do was feel that the world had collapsed on him. All those years, all the work come to so little because of some small defect, some lapse, some small problem—the kind of problem any big man could have. Groggily, on pure instinct learned from years of seeking appreciation, he smiled, signed the papers and said goodbye. All his will could do was improvise some weak little lies that would absolve him of responsibility. Make him triumphant his will could no longer seem to manage.

8. That Old Feeling of Feeling Old

The picture I get of my father's last months in New Jersey is of a man being forced out of what had actually been his life—of what, for better or worse, he'd sold his first beautiful dreams for. True, he'd cheated his business, crippled it while it was growing—but he'd worked, sweated and given his all in trying to make his lies realities. Defeated, he urged himself not to admit defeat. He wasn't going to be pushed out, he was retiring. His friends told him he was doing a wise thing. They patted him on the back. And so he even came to believe he was doing a wise thing—something only a big man could do. Everything was fine, the standard operation he was used to performing—except for one small detail. This time, he couldn't quite believe it. Almost, but not quite.

The reasons aren't hard to come by. Age was one thing. For a good part of over fifty years, he had carried his 320-pound bag of trouble around his bones. He'd had sickness after sickness. He'd been pierced by more needles, regulated by more conflicting pills and diets than any six sickly men. He'd made move after move that he'd had to make palatable. He'd had secret upon secret that he'd had to conceal by using every ruse he had at his command. Time was heavy on him. His fringe of hair was near white. His spindly legs felt the weight of his huge belly. Perhaps his will had been declining for years without his knowing. And the sudden change of circumstances, the change of horizons, of fears, of things to cover up had merely made the decline a little obvious.

Perhaps, if nothing had changed—if my uncle hadn't taken that deep breath and finally said what he'd had to say—my father's will could have trudged along out of force of habit, and he could have gone on for who knows how long?

As it was, for the first time in years, my father had the chance and overt need to sit down and consider his future. And with the tired, leaden weight of his past, he saw all the things he had to do: all the countless goodbyes, the trip, the fuss to make new friends, the efforts required to start out all over again. And in an instant, something inside him doubted his abilities and said, I can't do it, I'm too tired. And maybe in that instant he'd grown old.

The point is not that his will was dead; it was declining. It was becoming harder for him to shield himself from a heaviness and darkness of heart, harder for him to forget his actions, harder for him to maintain a good opinion of himself. Not that he couldn't rise to an occasion. He could and would for some time to come. It was just harder. And he couldn't sustain illusions long enough to fully turn apparent failures into triumphs. And having, in an instant, unconsciously doubted his will, he was no longer able to reject confusing, self-incriminating questions. He became lost in a maze of doubts, of cross-purposes, of regrets. Thus he imposed a double labor on his will. He aided, sped his own decline.

Desperately he tried to live as if he were as strong as ever. But with his gradual, slight, ever-imperceptible decline, he lost the ability to adapt, to change his manner of living, even as he planned to change most radically. He continued to fabricate lies when he could no longer feel guiltless for them. Nor could he still always construct them with the same ruthless logic. As he grew more desperate, as he doubted himself more, he exaggerated, made his lies bizarre, fantastic. He built huge castles on quicksand, trying to fool himself. But though he tried and sometimes almost succeeded, he—or one part of himself—could not believe his lies. He felt ill at ease with them. He no longer had faith in them. Brooding only made it worse, created additional strain, additional self-consciousness. And when this happened, he was no longer sure that any man believed him. Perhaps all this explains his failure at the accountant's office, and why he almost broke under the series of frustrations that were soon to sour his days.

9. California, Here He Comes

Like the man says, you can go on for years in the same circumstances, doing act after act like some machine. Change your circumstance, pull the old life out from under you, and, if you've grown old, it'll show. Had my father left Jersey an hour after his unhappy interview with the accountant; had he thrown himself immediately into a new life and occupied himself with all the problems that, in his easy chair, seemed so overwhelming, the decline of his will might have been prolonged over several years. But that's not what happened—is it even thinkable? A man in his position? A hundred things had to be done before he left—a hundred crippling chores. And in the meantime, he had so many chances to brood and worry, and (because of who he was) keep everything to himself.

The first blow was that our big magnate was Miami-bound no more. He'd dreaded this, and even after the fiasco at the accountant's he'd tried to convince my mother that he could find work in Miami. But he himself knew he would need work and Miami was not the place to find it. So his protest was weak, and in the end, he yielded.

Let me try to trace the pattern of his actions in the face of this defeat. It wasn't too hard for my father to place the change of destination in a flattering light. To himself he could say—as my mother'd said, in truth, of herself) that in California at least, he was loved. To his friends, he could say that he'd thought it over and Miami seemed like a place for old men. California, now, California was new. Young blood, a new world, things to see, things to do. After all, he'd say, I don't want to get old before my time. Besides (for he was no longer sure of himself and he had to press a bit hard), he wanted to be near his daughter and her family; he wanted to help them. Not that his son-in-law wasn't doing all right—his son-in-law a failure? But he just wanted to give him the benefit of his experience.

Saying all that blather was easy enough, but something in my father made him feel it wasn't convincing. He thought he detected a touch of scorn behind the smiling, nodding heads. He even wondered: had his brother told his friends about the business settlement? He scoffed at the idea, which didn't stop it from reappearing.

The next problem was a job, and not because our magnate was used to being active. Even my frugal mother was used to living on quite a bit more than twelve thousand a year. And she certainly realized there had to be money for the last years after that. You get used to money, even if you can't dangle your feet over the side of a Miami Beach swimming pool. Her beloved only son was already in college, and that was costing and would continue to cost. If I was a possible ace in the hole, an investment would have to be made even if part of the deal inevitably meant my transfer to the state u. I've already told you about. (You sure it's o.k. son? he would ask, because you know we want the best for you. Sure dad, I told him.)

My father had to know my mother was a doubly worried person because on the one hand, they had to watch their money; and on the other, they had to spend it. Great wielder of words and man of good will that he was, my father told her not to worry. Lots of his pals had connections of the West Coast. He'd have no trouble getting himself a nice, comfortable job. And because he couldn't really believe this, because that old thing in him kept on saying, who'd give you a job? At your age? Obese as you are? He struck back like a scared animal. When I say "job," I don't mean a hundred dollars a week. Why, a man of his abilities, a man of his experience, could make fifty thousand a year—with ease! Doing what he didn't know—maybe restaurant consulting, maybe public relations for something or other. Why, the more he thought of it, the more leaving the restaurant seemed to be a step out of the bush leagues. And feeling he hadn't convinced her, he said, why, his friends wouldn't let him down. Bobbie, and then Joe and Morrie—them and all the others—they'd work to see to it he got something big. But you've got to think big, feel big. So immediately he went from twenty-five to fifty cent cigars. And the following week he bought three custom-made suits.

But even with the world's finest cigar in his mouth, my father decided to play it safe. After all, wasn't he a practical man? He knew his friends had all sorts of California connections. But he couldn't very well put his hat in his hands and say, I need a job. He'd have to put it to his friends more subtly, carelessly—as if it really didn't make too much difference. His first step was over a period of days to complain of restlessness, to say it was bad for a man who'd worked all his life to just sit around. Next he'd say a man like me can't sit on his fat ass. When I get to California, I'll have to get a five day a week job or else I'll go crazy. Not that he would need it, mind you. No. He was fixed for life. But if I don't do something, I'll go out of my mind inside of a couple of weeks.

A few months before, he could have pulled it off gracefully. Because he would have believed it. But now, he didn't believe—and so he doubted if they did. He'd gotten a new ball and pawed the ground. But he was afraid to make a pitch. Several times he was on the verge. But maybe he'd perceive a bit of disinterest on the part of his listener. Maybe while he was trying to marshal his courage, his friend would go off on a different tack. Maybe the phone would ring. It wasn't an easy job. Because he couldn't bring it up more than once in a given conversation. A few months earlier he could have, and gotten away with it. But now it seemed a patronizing dead giveaway. Then too, he couldn't say it out of the blue, like, by the way, Bob, you don't know any one who could get me a job in California, do you? No, his listener had to be prepared; the rhythm of the talk had to be right. It all had to be said at the right moment, in the right context, when his listener had gotten involved in the sequence of deceits. It had to be part of a flow—a logical conclusion. Ideally, it would be volunteered without direct soliciting. It would be, say Sam, I've got a friend on the West Coast who might have just the thing for you. But what were the chances of that?

So the days passed by without my father getting any definite commitments. To my mother's queries, he'd answer something vague, like everything's under control or, don't worry, things'll be all right. Then he'd smile, his lips broadening so you couldn't tell whether it was from confidence or pain. He began to harbor resentments against his friends: they didn't give a damn when a man was down. But he couldn't say he was down, and that just showed you what kinds of friends they were really. He lit a cigar and backed off, realizing he hadn't even asked them yet. I'm just waiting for the right moment, he told himself. And when that moment came, everyone would see what kind of friends a man like him had.

But he wondered; he wondered and worried and brooded. For days he'd had the feeling that his friends were getting tired of his hedging; that they knew what he wanted but weren't interested. He was tired of trying to answer my mother, of trying to cook up excuses and only managing vague evasions. Time was dragging. The recklessness he had imagined in his scheme had become real. And even though he was full of dread about leaving, he wanted to go as soon as possible.

But there were so many things to be done. My mother was busy selling household odds and ends, getting different storage and shipment prices for her precious antique furniture which she loved and my father called junk. He urged her to hurry. She tried to explain, Sam, you can't just pick up and leave like a gypsy. Besides, he didn't have any definite commitments about jobs yet. Without understanding, he accepted it. He wedged himself into his easy chair. And as if he didn't have enough to worry about already, the life he brooded over gave him another swift kick.

10. Waiting for the Mail

Sam, my mother said, now we're starting a new life in California. I don't want you to keep things from me anymore. Now, we want a fresh start, so if there's any old debts, anything we haven't paid for yet, let me know now so we can take care of it and get it out of the way. He said there was nothing. Now I won't get mad if there is, she guaranteed. But let's start with the slate clean. I don't want to have to start paying when we first get to California.

Again he assured her there was nothing. He swore to God. And she dropped the matter for a time, only to bring it up again and again—haunt him with it. The funny thing was, he didn't really know. He'd played his cat-and-mouse game so long and so well that even he had lost track of his debts. He'd never bothered to straighten them out. If there was a way to find out it was at the restaurant. But that, he reflected sadly, was no longer his. Besides, he couldn't make a move that would arouse suspicion. Fact is, had my mother not brought them up, had, instead, my father uncovered unpaid debts of his own, he'd have probably handed them over to her without qualms and said, not without a touch of nobility, here, dear, so we can clean the deck, so when we get to California, we can start fresh. But alerted in this manner, my father was determined to find out if he had debts and, if so, hide them for as long as possible. With my mother hounding him, it preyed on his mind, gnawed at his brain—if only he knew, if only he'd thought of it before! One thing he did know: if there were debts, whoever held the papers knew he was leaving; and before he left for California, the bills would come in the mail.

So began my father's first period of *Waiting for the Postman*. I know of two other such times, both in California. One over a similar, related matter and the other over letters friends never had time to write. The most striking thing about all three of these periods was that my father no longer had even the faintest illusion of freedom. He was regulated by the local delivery schedule, the postal employees, the Postmaster General. The most tyrannical masters were my mother and time itself. My father had to watch his every move. He couldn't let my mother suspect he was waiting for something. He couldn't stare out the window waiting or run helter-skelter to the mailbox. Yet he couldn't let her go; nor could he protest if she did. And so his mornings were spent in a kind of dull, grinding terror until he had his paws clutched around the daily mail.

Then there were minutes of elation when what he dreaded wasn't there. But gradually, as the hours passed, the clouds would darken. Fear would grow, getting worse all the time throughout the day. Probably sometimes during the restless, troubled nights, he'd feel like talking to someone or even praying. At times she could hear him tiptoeing out of the bedroom and into the living room, where if she went to check on him, he'd quick pick up a book and pretend to be reading. But that's just the way it was the first couple of weeks. After that it got worse. I've come to the conclusion that dread and terror gave way to something new, something more insidious and pernicious: hope. Hope that what had to happen would, and soon. As a man cannot live with regret, so he cannot live with constant dread. He must give way until he practically begs doom to fall. Sometimes he works to bring it on.

I ask myself how could he take it all? All this strain and muffling it all——never screaming, never letting on, somehow digesting it so he could prepare a face to meet the faces. I'm sure there were moments—there must have been—moments when he contemplated death. True he was a great actor; and when he thought of death, he must have felt himself momentarily sanctified, martyred, ennobled. But it's hard to detect the actor in yourself, and some great performers have been fooled into suicide. I do know this for sure: my father's spirits were lower than I'd ever seen them.

For a time it seemed his will had completely slackened off or deserted him. I remember a night at our apartment when a group of uncles and aunts gathered to discuss the latest disaster that had befallen my mother's rich older brother, my Uncle Abe. A nice enough guy, but weak-livered, half-crazy and also pretty stupid, Abe, had been arrested for trying to pass a bum check. Abe had made a fortune as butcher, but he or maybe his family (Hell, maybe he had a mistress) always seemed to squander it away, and he was always getting into hot water. Usually they'd close him down for selling horsemeat, and his brothers would have to bring in an army of lawyers to bail him out. But this time, they'd caught him dead to rights trying to pass a bum check for an amount plenty big enough to figure as a heavy felony. What was his problem, we all wondered. And where would it all lead, now that he was probably bound for prison?

This was a big family disgrace, that was for sure. And all the relatives were sitting around, eating like wolves and moaning and groaning about the whole business, with my father kind of trying to play lead voice or cantor in a Kaddish-chanting chorus. I don't understand it, he said, a man like Abe, with a loving wife and such a good family... risking all their happiness and security... His voice trailed off and no one seemed to notice too much because everyone was talking all at once, each with his own theory about rich and crooked Uncle Abe. But my father had stopped, he'd made the connection. He sat in silence; his double chin sank into his chest. While in the room, the talk, the clattering of coffee cups continued.

11. Good News in a Letter

This is America. And the postman brings good news as well as bad. Though usually not all deep and lasting, when you look at it squarely. But who could hope to find essential, enduring happiness for the price of a first class stamp?

After nearly two weeks of waiting for doom in an envelope, my father received a letter that sent him on a comet, made him feel ten feet tall, and the greatest, most loved guy in the state of New Jersey. His friend Bob, who'd been off in L.A. on business, had bumped into an old crony (a nice guy, by the way, Sam, you'd like him) who'd recently moved to Southern California to take over the management of the sales division of an east coast-based distributor of what who knew or cared? And what do you think? This old crony says he's going on the road, but he'll be back in L.A. by late July, and he says for you to look him up around August 1.

Immediately my father acted as if he'd already signed an agreement—and in blood. Of course, there was no direct mention of a job, but what else could Bob mean by it? Hadn't my father hedged and hedged until there could be no doubt about what he was after? And wasn't it great of Bob to understand all that without making him come out and say it? Lately my mother'd been carping at him more than ever. The other night, she'd even said to him (in her usual calm), you're lying, Sam. You don't have any jobs lined up. Sam, you're lying! Well, she'll see if he was a liar now. Now that he had something definite—or almost definite, which was just as good, maybe better.

The little bit of doubt was productive because it spurred him on to create iron certainty and forced him to forge a fantasy designed to feed his confidence. No question he had a job just waiting for him. Wouldn't he be the perfect man to help introduce an east coast product? But wasn't it just like life that when it rains it pours? Because once having lined up one job, wouldn't you know it? Another one comes your way like a ripe plum waiting to be plucked?

So it was that his cousin Morrie tells him that there's an opening some sort of operation for La Something or Other Cigar company in Santa Monica. And Morrie's wife's cousin's best friend says he can set up a meeting with a key company rep that'll just about assure the sweetest little job a retiring restaurateur could ever want to have.

Now, this is a real problem, no? Just when Bob's bagged one job, another comes along. And suddenly instead of worrying to death about the grim future ahead, about the callousness of supposed friends, and even doom in an envelope, suddenly you've got to worry about not hurting your friend's feelings after he's gone out of his way. You've got to work out angles and strategies and moves to play one job offer against the other to get the best possible deal. But naturally he didn't want to be greedy, and he didn't want to worry my mother or anyone around him with all the complicated decisions a man like him had to make.

So, manly man that he was, he kept his admittedly happy source of new worries to himself, and merely told my mother that all the big offers simply showed they had nothing more to worry about in California and they should get ready to go as soon as possible. As for the debts, well, with one job or the other, he could take care of any that might surface—and my mother wouldn't mind because his job worries were over, weren't they? Besides, he almost came to believe, I don't think there are any debts. I was all worked up over nothing. With all the iron force he could muster, he hitched his wagon to the job business. He was going to believe in it no matter what. The fact that he was lulling my mother into a false sense of security failed to stop him for a moment.

Characteristically, he was quick to reinforce his fabrication all the more. All things considered, they couldn't hope to leave till the middle of June, close to three weeks away. So why don't we go up to Canada for a few days? My mother wasn't sure. All the things she had to do and him hardly helping at all. And then, how were they supposed to go? They didn't have a decent car. Which was just what he wanted her to say.

Wasn't it (for God's sake) about time they got one? You can't make it in L.A. without one, and why wait till they were there? Cars were cheaper in the east, and then they could start their new life just driving out and seeing every mile of that great country that had given them (and to which they had given) so much. But she was afraid. She knew what he'd always wanted. Well, after all, I'm entitled to some consideration. I let you have your way about California. She eyed him harshly. Well, I've never had a car of my own. Always a business car he shared with his brother. Aren't I entitled? I mean, a man's got to have some dignity. All right, she yielded ever so reluctantly. All right, but not exactly what you have in mind.

Then he ran down all the advantages of a Cadillac. The roominess, the comfort, the sense of well-being. And, he added tactfully, it'll hold up for years and still be beautiful. Why, they'd never have to get another car. And so he argued for hours saying what a fine thing it would be, what an eye-catcher. And of course, he'd need it for his job—yes, that was the ticket. He'd be traveling and mixing with big, important men. Could he take a big man out to dinner in a Chevy? He called upon his manhood, he called upon the free enterprise system and its manifest virtues. He did verbal somersaults. And he won.

Grudgingly of course. And now without his swearing he was sure about having a job and that he had no unpaid debts; for the weeks of leisure had been costing money and she hadn't been able to save as much as she wanted.

The day after that final, deciding talk on the subject, my father went in to sign the papers for his Cadillac. For he had already chosen it. He told my mother he'd looked all over town (just window-shopping, mind you) for the best buy, and he'd bartered the man down to a reasonable price. All this was untrue. Can you imagine my father bickering over a few hundred dollars? He'd gone to the nearest dealer, seen the car he liked and put down a deposit. That was the way a big man with a big job awaiting him in California did things.

Two minor concessions my father did make. First, he wanted to pay cash, but he acquiesced and flattered my mother's silly sense of insecurity. That is, my mother did not have all the thousands to put down. So he arranged a three-year combination insurance-payment plan, which, I am sure, is recorded somewhere as, dollar for dollar, one of the most profitable transactions an insurance company ever handled. The second concession was a little harder for him to take. He'd reserved a car with those high-class hubcaps and the special streamlined but elaborate thousand dollar gold front ornament, and these my mother would not have.

Now, a big man does not go back to a dealer and say, I've decided not to take... or even, my wife insists... But my father had to do it. And I must concede he came through ably and without too many complaints, at least at first. Later, his not having those little touches was to gnaw at him as the difference between himself and the truly big men.

But what allure did a Caddy have in those days to all those sons and daughters of migration, immigration, and exile? We're dealing with a holy mystery it would be blasphemous to violate. To my father (and probably even my mother), the Caddy was a poem, a rhapsody and in blue, a Pindaric ode to the realization of a life-long struggle, a beautiful hymn to more than fifty years of epic battle... What crimes, what blood of human sacrifice underpin the most profound and sublime myths?

I will be brief and prosaic. After five days of effortless driving though Canada in the newest and perhaps best loved member of our family, my father returned home to find awaiting him in the mailbox, two bills from two different banks totaling some thousands of dollars in debts contracted six years before. In an instant, they were mere debris for a late May breeze. That night, sometime after dinner, my father suffered an acute attack, the culprit being diagnosed by physicians who were qualified to know as the peptic ulcer.

12. The Deepest Shadows

All the deepest shadows of my father's life fell over him during those days in the hospital as he lay in his room despondent, hardly eating, hardly reacting, a subject for concern and mystery for the hospital staff and his own family. He was tired, he looked tired. His large body groaned under the treatment it had been forced to undergo, the weight it had been forced to bear. It's clear to me that all his lies were staring him in the face.

Lying in bed, my father knew: the job story had been a postponement of the inevitable—a mere trap by which he got through his days by committing himself and at least his wife to future disappointment and pain. He healed slowly, it seemed he wouldn't heal. He had no reason to heal. He was afraid, deathly afraid of exile in a strange land. Without belief in his dreams, he was at the edge of despair. Having lost belief in his dreams, he was lost. But though he saw what he'd done and who he was, he could not find a way to change. Nor could he hope to or want to. For where was he to find the resources within or without to break the bonds of a slavery that had been his only source of life and freedom? Tired, suddenly old at fifty-five, could he suddenly say, to hell with all I've been and done—I'm coming clean, I'm breaking with all the shit? And could this man who felt himself so old and defeated bear to face the astonished disillusioned stares at his confession? And having thrown over his old self, his old life, could have had the strength to make a new? Could he, after all that had happened and also, above all, after all he had come to believe and value, even find out where to begin? He felt he could not; hence he could not. And maybe it was when his despondency led him to accept this state of affairs that he began to recover. Maybe it was just at this point of resignation that he could begin the process of healing, getting off his back and out of bed, of going back into training, to play his old part in the drama which had been his life—play his part until the final curtain as best as his fading talents would allow.

Is this story an indictment, an attack? Maybe, well not even maybe. But it's not against him, never against him, great actor that he was, great trouper even in his lowest moments. No, the whole thing's about something else, but not him. How could I write against him? No matter what.

13. The Curtain Begins to Come Down

That final curtain came a month later, when my father finally healed. The departure date had been pushed ahead to the morning of July 1st. Those last days in Jersey must have whirled by in a blur of packing and farewell get-togethers. But with any break in the flow and churn of things, my father was now morose, wearily sitting in his big easy chair, just overwhelmed by life. Still recovering, he'd say when asked, and he'd strain his facial muscles into a lifeless smile. No sure job awaited him in California, my mother would find out about his debts. In the face of my mother's nervous farewell gaiety, and in the midst of beaming relatives, my father had to keep it all to himself—and smile.

But there was further twist that made it all the harder. He could take all the pain, even the inkling he had that his last years might well be lived in the knowledge of bitter failure and maybe even poverty. Maybe there was no way he could avoid all this, he was accepting it as the possible, even inevitable stream of his life, and finding ways to handle it. What did not seem acceptable, what disquieted him beyond measure was the silence of his big friends. All the time he'd been in the hospital, all the time of his convalescence, he hadn't seen any of them. Cards, yes—but nothing more. It seemed unthinkable they could forget him so quickly, write him off so effortlessly. And while he was still living among them. He wouldn't ask for a party, but not even a word of goodbye?

You see, he had to have this. With all his submission and resignation, he strangely asked for this last gift. Something in him begged for a final, perhaps meaningless affirmation. Maybe it was the hope that he could dupe himself again. More likely, it was the rhythm of the life inside him that had to be fulfilled. The great actor had to make his final flourish. In the years of oblivion and approaching death, my father had to have the memory of a last triumph, a great moment, something epitomizing the life, or at least the dream of life that he'd led on this earth. Nevertheless, on the eve of his departure, he sat motionless and near tears; and with all the absurd possibilities that could occur to him, he asked what he'd done to divest himself of some small but somehow supreme moment of triumph.

But this is the land of ironic fairy tales, of successes that are supposed to blur all failures. My father was not to be robbed of his moment, nor the big friends of their last act of good will. For while he was sitting in pained meditation, the friends gathered in the gala party room of what had been his own restaurant and prepared to give him the grand sendoff.

14. The Big Farewell

Of course it was a little messy. Everyone was to have gotten there by eight; half of them hadn't shown at nine. And the man who was to have instructed my mother to have my father at the restaurant had forgotten all about his job and gone on a pleasure junket to Havana. But what are these little things in memory? At 9:20, my father received a call telling him to come over at once. And he knew! His friends hadn't let him down. Not *his* friends. How foolish he'd been to doubt them. How crazy! In the nervous excitement, he put on a shirt, his shoes, a soiled tie. He brushed his narrow fringe of hair and shaved, making comic remarks like the ones he'd made in better days. All the way over to the restaurant, he rehearsed what he was going to do, rehearsed for the hundredth time the way he was going to thank them. For the last time, his will blazed as of old. He exuded confidence, joviality, bravado.

It was a party with all the trimmings, much like the ones he himself had catered for others. Hors d'oeuvres and spreads of all kinds, animal-shaped mayonnaise salads, and a huge gaudy tiered cake topped by the effigy of a rather obese bald-headed man, standing alongside a big, beautiful Cadillac. And below the cake, on the floor, a wide array of gifts, mysterious, wrapped in paper and ribbon all around their stupendous centerpiece: a bizarre red, white and blue plastic-boxed portable TV set.

The proceedings got under way, with the warm testimonies and wishes of those who were there, the telegrams from those unable to attend, and finally a billfold with cards conferring on my father honorary membership in the Elks, the Rotarians, the Kiwanians, the Lions and all the organizations that bespoke the glory that was New Jersey. Amusing anecdotes and heart-felt wishes rounded out the preliminaries. And then finally (what they'd all been waiting for), my father, humble, overwhelmed with nostalgia and joy, acknowledged the popular clamor and launched his obligatory words of thanks.

For twenty minutes he kept them in stitches. He talked of this tailor and that rabbi and even (for wasn't he American too?) the farmer's daughter. Then he grew solemn and evoked the history of Jews in the Old World and the New. He talked of ghettos and shtetls, pogroms and concentration camps. He spoke of poor persecuted Jews barely making it to cross the seas. He spoke of pushcarts and poverty in U.S. urban centers. He spoke of rich German Jews and poor Russian Jews and even poorer other Jews. He spoke of Commie, pinko and good American Jews. He spoke of Heifetz and Einstein, of Bennie Leonard and Barney Ross, Hank Greenberg, Al Rosen and Sid Gordon, and then, above all, the great masses of simple, honest small businessmen Jews: the ground for all the others, the salt of the earth who just tried to eke out a living for their dear ones and send their kids to college so they could in turn be a credit to their families and the country that had taken them in and given them so much. How many hardships had they endured? How many sacrifices had they made? But they'd survived the pogroms and gas chambers, they'd lived through the poverty and depression, they'd lived, survived and learned to thrive, feathering their nests, yes, but also building their synagogues, and sending their kids door to door to raise money for planting trees in the New Jewish Homeland.

And sure, of course, there were still lefties and pinkos among us, but less all the time, no? And it wasn't just that we thought of our own. Who more than we knew what discrimination and persecution and extermination really were, and we'd never forget, we'd always fight against them, not just for ourselves but for all, regardless if you were black, brown or blue. But even in this, we'd remained Jews even as we'd become Americans. We'd become *Jewish Americans, American Jews* now safe from old world tyrannies, and from radical temptations, now ready to forge the future in our city's suburbs or (the true frontiersmen of our time), now claiming the place we'd earned in the sun, vanguarding that great new caravan of so many going south toward Caribbean keys or west toward Pacific palisades.

Waxing ever more poetic and prophetic, he spoke of life and death and the riches of freedom and opportunity. How wonderful it was to live in this wonderful land of ours. How wonderful to have lived at this juncture in the history of humankind. He talked of the big, fabulous times with his big, fabulous friends. And then he talked of how life—life meant hellos and goodbyes. And yet he hoped and in his heart of hearts he *knew* that this wasn't the last he'd see of his friends. He'd be taking a trip back, in a year he said, to see if Milt'd lost weight and Jake'd finally fixed his garage door. And of course, of course, he was hopeful that all of them would be making their way out to the sunshine state sooner or later and they'd be guests in his home. But (his voice darkened) perhaps—life being what it was—there would never again be the closeness they all felt at this moment. Perhaps he would never see some of them again. Perhaps they would forget him and all they'd done together. And his friends clamored, no! no! And then the no's trailed off. The great actor paused and lit his cigar. No, he repeated. You are right, my friends. Who could really believe that? We're a communal god-fearing people. Others broke apart and went their lonely, separate ways, lost in the sea of life. But not them, not after what they'd been through—the suffering, the hard work, the good times, the good deeds, the Israel trees, the Rosenbergs.

No, friends, we shall never really part. It was just that California needs us, our people out there need us. It was our call to bring the old values of the east to the west. But that would not separate us, it would bring us together all the more—a people united by their past, united by their future. Always together, never apart, at peace with their god, at home in Israel and America, struggling together, making a better world together, now and tomorrow, for themselves and their children and their children's children, as they had done in the past, as they were doing in the present and as they would do in the future—together, forever!

A cheer, a great cheer. And then, with a tremor in his voice, a thanks from the bottom of his heart, and of course a thanks too from Sarah and all the family and well, not goodbye, but farewell!

And what could happen next? *For He's a Jolly Good Fellow* and *Auld Lang Syne*. And then the handshakes, the hugs, the backslapping. The booming voices, the smiling faces. The tears. As he made his way to the door, even his brother embraced him and murmured, good luck Sam. And then they made their way out to his car and helped him load in the gifts. He stepped behind the wheel and waved his hand a final time.

What an impression the car must have made that late June evening so late at night. What bigness, what beauty. What a ship to carry a big man across his big country! Before returning inside for their final drinks, the friends stood by silently until the huge red rear lights had followed the car around the corner some three hundred yards away and out of sight.

Book Two.

Another Way West

(The Son)

Part I. The Long Hot Summer

1. The Trip

Mel had traveled to California two summers before by plane; but when his parents told him they had decided move to California, he decided to cross the country by land but still beat them to the West Coast to spend a fine summer before returning Dartmouth for the 1958-59 academic year. He had brought his Mercury back with him at spring break; and now, the snow melted and mud the campus king, he trudged to the parking lot and took his car to a mechanic to prepare it for the trip. Then he put an ad on the dorm student center bulletin board and found two students willing to share driving expenses to California. For several days, he worked through complex and difficult finals, wrote on all the novels and the history of Europe—all the themes he most loved; and then, the car and his partners ready, he loaded in his belongings, loaded up the partners and their stuff, and, into the late afternoon, set off for Chicago and places south and west.

It was a rapid fire trip with no time to see monuments or vistas and not even much for talk, as the boys took shifts—two hours driving, two hours co-piloting, two hours sleeping and then driving again, the car given no respite, as they made their way through roads that all but melted the unrested tires as they chased after the late afternoon heat on their way toward the setting sun.

The boys skirted Chicago, headed down to St. Louis, and then, stopping for some barbecue, made their way on to Route 66, stopping only briefly so that one of the boys could say hello to his grandparents who ran a hamburger stand on the side of the road by their farm. Loading up on the burgers, they were distant observers of a conversation they could not hear between the boy and his grandparents, older people reticent in expressing their feelings, seemingly as dry as wheat and corn—American Gothic roadside. Then it was off further down the road, somehow following the Joads, Mel mused, when they passed through and beyond Oklahoma, past the panhandle and that bit of Texas and then, passing Gallup, New Mexico, going on to the vast dessert stretch that would lead to Barstow, San Bernardino and Los Angeles, rolling up to Santa Barbara to leave off the first partner at the door of his house, and then onto the Alhambra home of the second, before, now alone for the first time in four days, he spent hours running into one cul de sac after another until he finally entered the tiny street of his sister and brother-in-law, was greeted with great pleasure, treated to a lemonade and a lawn chair, where he finally drifted off to sleep in the early afternoon sun and smog of Southern California.

He slept deeply without a worry, knowing that when he awoke his summer stay in California would begin, not knowing that in fact, he would never return east except for a visit or two as his new life took its course.

2. First Friends and A One Night Stand

He had made some friends on his first trip, starting with Florence, the second cousin of his brother-law Elmer, who introduced Mel to her son Larry, who in turn became his first close friend in California, and whose friends also became his friends. During that first trip, he had visited his first drive-ins, cruised Hollywood Boulevard chasing girls, as they went about their way. There was Mike Lerner who seemed to talk about sex more than any one Mel ever knew; there was Dan Levine, a physicist-to-be, giving his all to be just a young male before physics and his girlfriend grabbed him by the throat and started to make him the competitive and disappointed man he seemed programed to become. Mel remembered these boys and their pride in being young and Jewish in this time and place. He remembered lolling about in Larry's tiny but wonderful circular pool; he remembered the beach outings and the girls who went along; and above all, he remembered the trip these friends invited him to, to Lake Arrowhead, where they canoed, drank much beer and skinny-dipped in the bluest and clearest of blue clear waters. The friendships were begun, and Mel looked forward to renewing them as soon as possible, especially since he admired Larry as his guide, mentor and indeed life philosopher. But on calling him, he found that his friends were taking summer school classes in Berkeley, and Larry himself would be leaving the next day for a trip to Mexico that would keep him away for much of the summer.

"One thing I can do for you," he said, "is set you up for the hottest date you might ever want—and she just might make your whole summer. I only wish you'd told me you were coming, and I would've made other plans too. Maybe I wouldn't have gone away."

Disappointed with Larry's imminent departure, and now lonely in his sister's house, with her, his nieces and brother-in-law, Mel was eager to call the girl. And when he did, what a deep caressing voice she had. How well they connected on the phone, with him joking but of course fearful about how she'd deal with his bald head, his slight paunch, and general shabbiness (for Dartmouth had done little for his sense of fashion). They hit it off so well, that he almost forgot to make a date with her, dazzled by the low sexiness of her voice, the vibrato of her laugh and signs, but finally he made the date planning a night based on the little he knew of L.A. in his first weeks there. She expressed eagerness to meet him, and all but insisted on meeting him sooner than he had proposed, so indeed he would see her the next night.

Off he went, showered, and shaved; and when he got to her house, he rang the bell and all but swooned at the beauty of the girl who met him at the door. She was a Jewish Mediterranean dream, with shining, dangerous eyes, her voice even lower in person than on the phone. In the short time he'd been in L.A., he'd already found a local jazz station and jotted down the addresses of a few places and decided to take her to the Renaissance Club on Sunset Boulevard, because the new Miles Davis sextet was playing there. The place had a beautiful view south, down into Beverley Hills, convenient parking and was the most intimate club one could possibly find. She seemed overwhelmed by his choice, as they took a table near the musicians and fell completely in with their playing—Red Garland, Cannonball and Nat Adderley, Paul Chambers, Philly Joe Jones, and John Coltrane. What an incredible sound, what explorations, with Coltrane on his way to becoming fully Coltrane. Then between sets came a mime artist, Bernard Bragg, who acted out suggestions from the audience. "Joe DiMaggio and Arthur Miller courting Marylin Monroe," he wrote on the pad which circulated among the public.

And sure enough the mime artist chose this skit, flexing his muscles like the discus thrower, become pensive like "The Thinker," becoming the queen of sex appeal with pouting lips and inviting gestures, as the war of brains and brawn with beauty raged on.

His date was overwhelmed, as they shared a small, delicious pizza and a pair of drinks. "What a great suggestion for an impov," she told him.

Then came the band again, and they finally left the club filled with the joy of performance, making their way back to Burbank and her house. Then on arriving, he turned off the motor to listen to her explaining all so suddenly that she like Larry and the others had made plans for the summer, and how sad when they'd just met. He lamented the fact and admitted he was totally smitten with her.

"I'm so into you," he said. "I just wonder if you'd stay with me a few minutes just to make up for the summer nights we won't be able to spend together."

"Yes," she half-whispered, "but just for a couple of minutes."

It was a kind of down payment on the fall, when she came back. He dared not say that he'd be gone by then back to Dartmouth, and agreed to all she said, and then kissed and intertwined his tongue with hers as their bodies throbbed and expressed all that might have come to be, perhaps exaggerating in their anticipation, until their aching embraces peaked and demanded added levels, when she suddenly turned from him.

"Enough!" she said. "Things are going too far, too fast'; and she sprang from the car, running toward the front door of his house, only turning back when she arrived and then waving to him before she opened the door and he drove away, wondering if he would ever but all but knowing he would never see her again.

3. Sandy and the Summer Turn

So now he was alone in L.A listening to jazz and wondering what to do with his summer until his parents arrived and set up house in the Valley. Day followed day and the most he could get himself to do was pool his last moneys to repair the car from the horrendous beating it had taken on the trip. Meantime, his sister suggested that perhaps he should enroll in UCLA's summer school program, so he'd have something to do and at least move along with his education. He enrolled in a chemistry class to get rid of one of the horrible science requirements which had made his life less than happy at Dartmouth. Each day he left the house at 8 and drove over the canyons separating the Valley from L.A. proper. Finding his parking place, he attended a three hour class that made life almost unbearable those summer mornings. However, after a few days, his brother-in-law Elmer informed him that a friend of his from the Rodef Sholem Synagogue had a niece visiting from Brooklyn who was also thinking of enrolling late at UCLA but had no transportation.

The friend was willing to pay for the gas for him to round trip his niece to UCLA. To be sure, it was a long trip north from Van Nuys to Granada Hills and the girl's house before they even began the trip south to UCLA. But Mel, having nothing to do but play with his young nieces, and still waiting for his parents to arrive from a trek which had turned into a grand site-seeing tour, decided he should take on this role.

When he met the girl, he was glad enough about his decision. There she was with her chubby, pretty face framed by bangs, her eyes almond, her smell fresh and girlish. Not much given to talk she answered his friendly questions oh so briefly as off they went each day to the campus, him parking the car, each going to separate classes, agreeing to meet at an outdoor campus café before returning home. It was another long drive from his house to hers, over the canyon and then off to the UCLA parking lot. The return was equally long, and sometimes longer, because with time they decided to go to the beach, before going home to study and get ready for the next day's routine.

Something just didn't happen. He couldn't say he wasn't attracted and sometimes he even sensed she might be warming toward him. The weather heated up in July, and their retreats down Sunset to Will Rogers Beach became more frequent. They pretended to do their homework, but more often they just lolled around, looking out to sea, running and playing in the cold but bearable surf. Once he found himself meditating on her ample breasts, her broad-beams. Another time he found himself fantasizing mounting her, kissing her pretty face, laughing with her as they did now, but with intimacy and the stirrings of desire and even love. But though she seemed somehow interested, he couldn't claim to be really taken. He never asked her out on an evening or weekend date. He never asked her out on a weekend adventure. They never explored their new turf together, but just repeated the same old routines over and over again. Sometimes he asked himself what was wrong, why didn't he advance, even when he admitted that he was attracted after all. Was it because she was going back to Brooklyn at the end of the summer, and he'd be off at Dartmouth with a different social world? Was it that she with Brooklyn Jewish accent and unintellectual manner seemed now too simple for him, he the winner of his ivy league freshman writing contest?

He would simply ask what she was doing for the weekend and felt almost relieved to find that her uncle had made plans for her to go here or there. And so he had no obligation, no necessity. And simply called late Sunday evening to confirm his pickup the next day. Meanwhile the chemistry class was impossible; he hated every minute in class, and just waited for it to end, happy to be with her, but unwilling to make a move that would at all draw them together. And sure enough, his folks finally arrived, staying at a motel with their fellow travelers, Aunt Mollie and Uncle Frank, eager to tell all those on Stagg street about their many tourist adventures on their way, and eager to find an apartment to get out of their hotel, eager to see their grandchildren and eager too to move into a place of their own. Sure enough, they found an apartment, but without a swimming pool. As long as Molly and Frank were visiting, Mel made no move from his sister's house. But he had to be with his parents almost on a daily basis, which cramped his free time even if he'd wanted to change his relationship with Sandy. Then too, even with Mollie and Frank present, the family reality became clearer, as Mel found that his parents weren't as well off as he'd imagined, and the question of his return to Dartmouth suddenly came into doubt.

"Don't you understand?" his sister told him. "It's about time you realized that our father has a terrible gambling habit, he embezzled thousands from the business to pay off debts, and so he didn't get such a great deal when he sold out his share. Now he's here, living on the payments, and what chances is he going to have on the job market, at his age and with his kidneys and everything else? So wake up, boy, andÓ see where that leaves you and what you're going to do."

Confronting his parents, he heard them committed to his returning to Dartmouth; but looking at their faces, he could see this would be an enormous strain. He wrote the college, asking for a scholarship. They granted him $300 which didn't pay his plane fare, and he began to realize that his ivy league days were probably over.

It was then that the chemistry class was winding down and he felt more tension to step up his relationship with Sandy. But he couldn't seem to do it. She was pretty enough, and he was young enough, but virgin, yes still virgin that he was, the more tentative he became as he approached her. Besides there seemed no mystique about it. She was just a nice sweet Jewish girl from Brooklyn, perhaps more worldly and experienced than he could imagine, but he couldn't even get himself to talk about such things to her, couldn't seem to advance beyond a kiss, making it clear they were summer friends and no more, though yes sometimes somehow suggesting that more might come of this after all.

The last day of classes, they drove to her home in silence, neither seeming to know what to say. Finally he asked her how much longer she'd be in California, and she told him she still had a few weeks. He then lied and told her he'd be tied up a few days but would then call her to see if they could get together. She said that was fine since her uncle and family were planning to take her up to spend some time in San Francisco. Mel sighed at the respite, took her in his arms, and kissed her.

"You were great this summer, I don't think I could've gotten through that chemistry course without you."

"Couldn't have gotten through mine either," \she said, giving him a sweet little kiss of her own. And then she, her bangs and broad-beamed body were out of his car, and he made his way home.

There, mid-summer, Mel focused on his situation in Southern California. His father's previously unknown life now came to the surface and haunted his every thought, his every projected move. The option of returning to Dartmouth began to fade, and the thought of staying in the L.A. area wasn't very appealing, since the only friends he knew, so absent to him this summer, would be transferring to Berkeley in the fall. Did his family have enough resources to help him with out-of-state fees and the rest? Should this be the next move in his life?

In the meantime, he decided that if he were going to be a writer, he'd better start writing again, developing a narrative, much influenced by Camus's *The Stranger*, and entitled *Disease*. It was the story of a young man who suddenly realizes he is suffering a terminal illness in silence, in his room, no longer attending classes, keeping a journal, and getting ready to die his young death. In a central scene, his father comes to visit him and attempts to exercise his moral, patriarchal authority to snap his son out of his isolation and seek help or indeed find out if he was really ill. The boy refuses to oblige and accuses his father of all kinds of unnamable crimes, rejecting his right to authority and, finally alone, preparing himself for the final stages of his illness. Falling asleep, he dreams of a boy who has crazed, musical flights on the piano, somehow parallel to the boy in Lawrence's "The Rocking Horse Winner," and who, discovering some horrendous family secret, goes down the stairs and hacks the piano to pieces. The story ends with the boy committed to an asylum where he continues writing his journal about being in school. All of this was not so much like Camus after all. Here, the protagonist's lack of prescribed affect was not due to his openness to impulses from the world, as much as an expression of feelings repressed out of pain and a sense of betrayal.

And what was the father's crime leading to the disease of the son? This remained unclear, though in this long hot summer, the rising current of feeling had everything to do with his father's moral failure and the creeping paralysis that came on the son.

Indeed, writing the story and living the sense of reduced life possibilities were part of the same process that kept Mel virtually locked in his new California bedroom as July gave way to August.

Meanwhile he kept pushing Sandy deeper into his pocket, knowing he should call her but not wanting to do it and dreading a call of her own. Both the novel writing and the sense of angst it was raising in him prevented him from focusing on his future, let alone his pathetic and undeveloped summer romance. Indeed, Mel began to feel his youth smothered in anguish and doubt. And sure enough when he was feeling his worst and feeling least able to open toward a girl, no matter how cute or nice or bright or sexy he might find her, that very time, that very Monday after another weekend of avoiding her, Sandy finally called him.

"Is this Mel?" she asked.

"Hi Sandy, that's really a good question, because I've been so out of it. I've been meaning to call you but I didn't want you to have to share my depression. How was your trip?"

"My trip was fine, but that was more than two weeks ago. And now the summer's almost over…"

"I'm so sorry—it's just a lot of family problems got me rolling and then I've been trying to write it all in a fiction, and that's taken me days and days…"

"Oh," she answered glumly, and then listened to his silence at the other end of the line. "I guess that takes a lot of time and concentration," she offered finally.

"Yes," he answered, "You kind of choose between living and writing about life."

"Yes, I guess it doesn't leave much time for seeing a Brooklyn Jewish girl who's leaving soon."

"No," he answered quickly, "Of course I've time. Let's make a day of it. Let's go to all the places around L.A. we didn't get to go to before."

"All right," she said, perking up with his upbeat words. "Yes!"

"When would be good for you?" he asked.

"Well soon, because I'm leaving next Sunday."

"Next Sunday," he answered glumly. "I didn't realize you were leaving so soon."

"Well, but don't take it so bad," she said, seemingly encouraged a little by his tone, "We can still see each other when we're both in the east."

"Sandy, I'm not going back east," he blurted out. "My folks can't afford it, and I certainly can't. Looks like I'll be going to school here or up in the bay area."

"Oh," she replied, apparently stunned. "Well maybe it doesn't make much sense for us to see each other after all," she blurted out. "Besides, if you couldn't see me when you were just a few miles away, you probably weren't going to see me in the east anyway."

"Maybe," he confessed. And there was another long pause.

"You really don't want to see me before I go…" she asked with the most forlorn of voices.

"I guess not," he found himself admitting. "What would be the sense? We just might find ourselves getting really close when there's no sense or future in it."

"Yes," she admitted. "But you didn't like me really even a little bit."

"It wasn't that," he said, realizing they'd shifted to the past tense. "I liked you a whole lot. It was just a bad, confusing time for me."

"I guess," she answered. And there was another silence. "So this is it?" she asked.

"I guess so," he answered.

"Well… have a good life."

"You too, Sandy, have a wonderful life full of love and hope."

"You too," she said, and then she hang up.

How many times did Mel think of calling her back but he never did? The day of her departure came, then the hour, and to the very end he thought of calling and then it was too late.

4. Larry, Red and Off to Berkeley

Sandy was gone and that was the end of it. It was only over the years that Mel regretted his summary dismissal of his summer friend. Into his seventies, he never fully understood why he had treated her as he did, why he had thrown away this great opportunity in his summer life. Probably the pain over his father and his new resolve to escape all the problems and disappointment of the east to make a new life in the west was what explained most of it. Sandy perhaps was not his image of the right and wonderful Jewish girl. Whatever the cause, it all failed, and, then, in his twentieth, virginal year, during this long, hot summer, he was thoroughly alone, reading over a short novel draft that didn't make sense or come alive, wondering if he could ever become a writer, at the same time as each day, sitting with his parents with their own problems he poured through *The L.A. Times* want ads to see if there might be some writing apprenticeship he could find with one of the studios.

"You need to prepare a portfolio," his father told him, "And I don't think you've got enough to show. You better get back to school, get some education and build that portfolio."

And Mel knew that however he might now wish to disqualify his father, he was right about all this. So what was he do to fill his final days before the new school year? Before he could decide what to do, he received a phone call from one of his last high school friends, Red Feldman, the cousin of his high school love, who had somehow bonded with Mel in his last summer before Mel he went off to Dartmouth and Red went off to medical school in Rochester.

"How'd you find me?" Mel asked in great surprise.

"I called up your uncle at the restaurant and he gave me your folks' number."

"Great," said Mel.

"Listen," Red said, "I've got a couple of weeks before I have to get ready for Rochester, and I was wondering if I might be able to come out so you can show me all you can about Southern California."

"Great!" Mel repeated, though he knew this would spell the end of his writing efforts. Still, Red was a bright and special friend. "I haven't seen too much or done too much, but we can explore together," he suggested.

Red said he would check out flights and let him know what his options were for coming, and Mel got his mother to agree to his getting an extra mattress, so his friend had some place to sleep. He then raced to write a play, perhaps a step toward a film script, and somehow related to his *Disease* manuscript— a text called, "Searching for Dr. Moran," about a sick young man's frustrated and ever-fruitless search for a doctor who has somehow achieved fame because of this ability to cure mysterious illnesses. He finished part of the first draft and then realized how empty the play was and abandoned it, just as Red made it to the Burbank airport, and Mel whisked him over to his family's new apartment. There was little doubt in Mel's mind that his first interest in this friend stemmed from his kinship with Ellen. He knew he offered no road back to her, but even the slightest and vaguest reference to her and her life, kept Mel alive and ready. But then too, their friendship had grown in relation to their mutual interests and hopes, and it had extended even during their first year of college.

Now, seeing his red-haired friend, Mel felt a lift and could take on the role of a young male showing his pal around. And that indeed is what they did, traveling around L.A., going to the beach, taking in some jazz clubs in the evenings.

Mel's favorite spot remained the Renaissance, but they also heard of other places on a local jazz station which led them into Black Los Angeles and even Mexican L.A. as they tracked down local groups and venues. As the days went by, Red asked to read some of Mel's writing, so he showed him the two pieces he'd published in *The Dartmouth Quarterly*, though he held back on *Disease* and *Searching for Dr. Moran*. Red raved about *All the World in Bibleland*. This is great, he said half through it. It's a great idea and you're having lots of fun, and your readers are too. Very original very avant garde," he gushed. But then he took "Shadows" into the bathroom and came out with a sour face.

"This is really lousy," he said, "Sentimental tripe, not worthy of a career, worthy of nothing. Why did you want to publish this?"

Mel was devastated, and yet he knew his friend knew what he was talking about. The fact is he'd written little enough—a story about a jazz musician, Clint Lauder (sounded more like a cowboy), who kills himself in his hotel room, another about Greenwich Village bohemians and little else.

And yet *Quarterly* editor, David Viscott had asked him for something, and this piece he'd really written in high school was all he had to show.

Red had just finished a summer course on American fiction with the famous poet, Allen Tate, who was filled with opinions about style and the novel—how fundamental was Henry James, how fine Hemingway, how graceful F. Scott Fitzgerald, how brilliant Faulkner and how competent as a novelist was Penn Warren. How powerful but crude Dreiser, Lewis and a whole smarm of young writers leading to James Jones and Norman Mailer. Red questioned Mel's taste, his sense of pride, his direction. He even got into his jazz world.

"Much of this West Coast stuff, Chet Baker, Shelly Mann, Mulligan, Getz and the rest, is not worth a nickel. Only Brubeck has something, especially with Paul Desmond, but you probably don't think that's even jazz. I took a couple of records by Brubeck and the Modern Jazz Quartet to a dinner thing I went to at the house of Rudolph Serkin. I played them for him, and he said it wasn't bad but just couldn't compare to classical music. It just wasn't sharp enough, was too superficial, too hit and miss. And I guess that's the difference between your play and your story. The play's like classical music, and the story's like a cheap pretentious jazz piece."

Mel felt so deflated, he didn't know what to say. Had this supposed friend come to the west coast to torment him and make him doubt all that might be about his new life and his future. Still, it was good to be accompanied in this last phase of his summer. For indeed things were winding down.

He phoned Larry, who'd just come back from Mexico, had gone directly up to the Bay area, and said, "Look, I think it'd be great if you came up to Berkeley to see if this would work for you better than UCLA. I think Mike's roommate's leaving so you might be able to share an apartment with him even for a short time. But why don't you come up and talk to the administration about fees and all, see if they can waive the out-of-state fees and if you can still get in for the fall. Meanwhile you can crash at my place."

"Is it ok if I come up with a friend?"

"Male or female?" Larry asked.

"Male," Mel said glumly.

"Too bad, but no problem," said Larry. And the dates were set.

Red was thrilled by this new adventure as they said goodbye to Mel's parents and loaded Mel's Mercury for the trip north. They took the highway through alfalfa, cows, and soy. They got to Berkeley and called Larry, who said he'd gone to a hospital sick with dysentery, but that he'd left the key to his apartment with the manager, who was supposed to give it to Mel on request.

"This is worse than *Searching for Dr. Moran*," Mel told himself. But in a way he was glad that he and Red would have the run of the place for a few days. First they made their way around Telegraph Avenue, into and out of bookstores and records shops, Kips and other burger places, La Val's pizzeria on the northside and then the campus itself. They walked onto Dwinelle Plaza up toward the Campanile and then over to the river, exploring what would be Mel's new home. Mel entered the administration building and presented his credentials for transfer. They seemed not so overly impressed by his ivy league year, accepted his summer school class at UCLA and made it clear he would have to pay the out-of-stay-fee at least for a year. Out he came and the two headed for their first trip across the bay to San Francisco. The sun shone and all looked glorious as they rode around downtown, over to Fisherman's wharf, up to Coit Tower and out to the ocean, wheeling around, checking their tourist map and finally settling in on North Beach, to visit the City Lights Bookstore and other key spots that had become so famous in the previous decade.

They settled into an old-fashioned Italian eatery and ate a seven-course meal that never seemed to stop and cost something like $3.00 including a carafe of basic wine. Afterwards, they walked over to the Wine Cellar, where the jazz blared and the crowd roared.

"What a great town," Red said. "What a neat place to live—in Berkeley or here! Compare that to Rochester or Dartmouth!"

Mel couldn't fail to agree. There was no reason to doubt that the next phase of his life would not be in the winter cold of Dartmouth or the summer heat of L.A. Here there was theater, jazz and a gorgeous city, a little Manhattan, he thought, for him to discover and savor. The young men drove across the Golden Gate Bridge and stopped for a drink in Sausalito before taking a circuitous route than led them back toward Oakland and then Berkeley once again. Mel called Dan Levine and found that he needed a roommate and yes, he could move in in two days.

Then it was time to take Red to the airport, only to find that his friend had missed his plane, but then only to watch Red, a young man from a world of money that Mel had never known, cavalierly purchase a replacement ticket for over $400—more than Mel's trip would have cost for a year he wasn't going to be able to afford at Dartmouth.

Red talked to Mel about his dreams of being a doctor but ending also by being a writer like Chekhov or William Carlos Williams. "But as for you, my fine young Yeats," he joked. "Keep out of 'Shadows.'" The friends parted, planning to meet up the following summer, but they were never to communicate again in the more than sixty years which followed.

Just a few days later, returning to North Beach and walking down Green Street once again, Mel spied a familiar figure coming his way—slim as he was at Dartmouth, looking ever the poet in his unmatching nicker socks: it was Alden Van Buskirk, the brilliant student poet he'd met when he joined *Dartmouth Quarterly* and the coalition against pro-segregation poet David Wang.

"Alden!" Mel exclaimed. "What are you doing here?"

"Had to leave Dartmouth, my friend, camping here with some Beat friends, and writing up a storm."

"Well I guess I had to leave too," said Mel. "It was just too awful there except for you and just a few others."

"Yeah, well maybe you can get with us here," Van Buskirk offered. And he gave Mel a telephone number where he could be reached. But when Mel called a few days later, he was told that Buskirk had left his residence without leaving a forwarding address.

Only in 2012 did Mel look for him on Google, to find that he had died only two years after their encounter, leaving a volume of poetry with an intro. by Allen Ginsberg that had risen in critical approval some forty years after his death. So it was that Mel began his Bay area life with another door closed from the start, sorry that Red had left and that he couldn't find Alden but determined to make his way in his new world.

Part II. Digging In, Breaking Up and Breaking Down (1958-59)

1. Fall Plays, Sylvia and Eileen

So now he moved into his new room in the apartment he was to share this fall. In the days before classes, he got used to the relative crudeness of the place, the frequent trysts of his roommate and his girlfriend, always seeming to return from some tennis match or other, making love and then studying together as the most prim and proper couple in the world. It was clear to him that Levine was no longer the carefree friend of a high school summer, but now part of a boorish twosome who only put up with him because he helped pay the rent. Now, lonely and horny, he had to put up with the grunts and groans not only of this couple, but those of a rather well-known campus Marxist philosopher and his wife upstairs from his own apartment.

So Mel began his life as a student in Berkeley taking second year classes in World and British literature, French, Air Force ROTC (a required course) and most importantly, two advanced classes in dramatic theory and playwrighting. The whole thing excited him, especially the drama classes, because his great passion was dramatic literature, and he was constantly devouring play scripts. And the professor, Marvin Rosenberg, was a fine Jewish-American scholar who taught his students to see plays as structured on ritual from ancient times to the present century, and who taught them the value of performance in interpretation and creation. Few of the students in his classes grasped the major direction of his work (the moment by moment comparative look at performance); but even this class, with its focus on Francis Fergusson's *Idea of a Theater*, was overshadowed by the great adventure of creation in Rosenburg's other class, where students wrote plays that were immediately acted out by student actors and directors.

The first assignment was to write a play based on a story, and Mel went to town on Kafka's "A Hunger Artist," producing an overelaborate circus romp that was just so elongated and freewheeling that it thoroughly confused the actors working on it. (Later he would condense and condense it into a playable version that would actually win a playwriting contest and be produced). Then Mel tried to make a kind of dull, realistic play of his summer camp experience, and as a counterweight, he tried to develop a fairy-tale play, "A Name, A Tune, a Country," that he would work on without much success over the next several years.

Mel loved both classes with Rosenberg, which he felt gave him a special place in his second college year. But his ROTC course was just prior to these drama sessions, which meant that he who admired the beats and all things *avant garde* had to show up to class wearing his uniform. Attempting to look breezy, and impress some imagined girl or other, he left his tie loose; and one day an Airforce ROTC hotshot stopped him going into a class at Wheeler Hall, scandalized by his disrespect of uniform and taking down his name to report to the top brass on campus. Soon he received a reprimand from the Air Force staff; and without knowing it, he had taken his first step toward his later inability to continue at UC Berkeley.

Beyond that, all he can remember was his growing friendship with a young Black student in his class, his first and near-lifetime friend, Jay Wright, a former Mexican League ballplayer and G.I. who took the drama and creative playwrighting classes with him and who intently wrote out draft after draft of his plays in the most elegant handwriting possible. To Mel, Jay was a fine older friend, a mentor steering him toward writing, even though Mel felt that Jay lacked the fiery imagination and energy needed for great theater, and thought, wrongly, that he himself was a much greater, if undisciplined talent.

Jay washed dishes in the International House with a bright and crazy young poet, Michael McClure, who would later write the 60s camp tour de force, *McBird* in which LBJ, egged on by his wife, Lady Bird, murders JFK. But at that time, he was best known for having a python residing in the bathtub of his apartment. Jay invited Mel to a reading of Michael's early work and introduced him to the creative writing group formed by another student, Dianne Wakoski. They urged Mel to read some work of his own, and Mel could not but help hear the murmuring, "How awful, how useless." He never came back, though he persisted in believing there was some good writing in him, but maybe not in fiction. Instead, Mel clung to his hopes in theater, often allowing himself to be lured into after-class talk sessions with Jay and others. But even though he was drawn to the theater girls, the attraction came too late because he had already started dating a young Jewish student he had found in a film class he'd decided to audit—Sylvia Lachter, with short brown hair, a soft, Jewish body, and breasts that spoke to her name. "Who is Sylvia?" he intoned to himself, dreaming of the totally beautiful he finally invited out to a foreign movie or two and convinced himself that she was his ultimate true love.

Of course ,there wasn't too much time for dating, as they were both involved so much with their classes. Each week, he read the enormous assignments from his world literature class from Cervantes and Molière to Kafka and Beckett. One week for *Père Goriot*, another for *War and Peace*, as the class went on and on. For British literature, he studied with a snide but brilliant Brooklyn-bred Jewish professor, who seemed to like the fact that he had a young wannabe writer in his class—a *Landsman* he could humiliate perhaps to show his students that he was above any vulgar ethnic predilections. "That was a lousy paper," he declared to Mel in front of the entire class, scornfully returning what Mel thought was a fairly thorough critique of the pessimism pervading *King Lear*.

Another Jewish professor, Arthur Runter, bitter and antagonistic, barely taught him any French, but gave him lessons in how not to teach or treat your students. Still, the worst was ROTC, with its protocols and demands, its marching and posing.

Only after a heavy week did he see Sylvia on Friday or Saturday, often crossing the bay to see the likes of Monk, Miles or Anita O'Day when they came to town to play at the Black Hawk. All seemed to go well with her, with kisses and embraces advancing, with her ever so flirtatious, her checks and lips glowing from her makeup. What he most hated, however, was picking her up at a place she shared with an older woman, Margaret, who seemed more like an aunt or mother and seemed to find him totally lacking in interest. He tried to charm her but it was no good. Around her he felt bald, fat clumsy and stupid. She dismissed him with the most minimal smile, especially bemused by Mel's interest in a writer who changed men into bugs and sexual obsession into literature.

"Have you no interest in politics?" she asked, as Sylvia listened intently, seeming to agree. "Can't you see how important things are happening every day, how we have to fight McCarthyism even after McCarthy."

Mel nodded. "Yes, he said, "but right now I'm into the writing and I guess I need to do what I need to do."

"I see," said Margaret, "well good luck, I'm sure what you say is true for all of us," she said slyly, while Sylvia looked on.

Meantime, his friendship with. He couldn't understand Larry's relationship with a very waspish and not very pretty woman named Kara. Soon they were living together, and they'd invite him over for a weekend lunch or dinner. But Larry seemed somehow lost in a relationship with a woman he didn't love; he grew less and less communicative, less the friend he'd been early on. And soon, somehow, Kara grew on Mel, until she became the older woman who gave him some woman advice from time to time, especially when Larry wasn't around.

The fall rattled on, with Mel absorbed in his readings, and above all his dramatic theory and playwriting classes, his world with Jay and the other theater students. Then one day he went to a session of student-run skits, starting with Greek drama parodies and onto other things at the Dwinnelle Little Theatre; and there he saw that other girl who began to attract him even as he as he was drawn more and more to Sylvia.

This new flame was on stage playing Jocasta—her passions high, her histrionics at the max. She dominated the stage and seemed every inch a queen in agony for her Oedipus and Oedipal tie, until, young fool that he was, Mel finally realized it was all a high camp farce, as Jocasta came to know that the doll boy she'd been dallying with was indeed her son. Recoiling from her initial horror and hijinks, she began singing country 'n western style that incest wasn't so bad so long as you kept it in the family.

He didn't fall in love with her then and there, but he certainly found her fascinating from the start. Still, he was in love with Sylvia and tried to put aside this surge of newer feelings. It was just a thing, he convinced himself. It was the first time that he'd sat in on a student rehearsal and he was overwhelmed by the thought that these great young actors might soon act in one of his plays.

The director, British-handsome with golden hair and brazen neck scarf, seeming to act his part better than he could actually direct, soon halted the nonsense and then called on her to act the part of Laura with the gentleman caller, and after her most delicate performance of the scene, so superior to Jane Wyman or even Julie Haydon, he called on her to play Amanda with a younger but hypersensitive Laura acting the part as Eileen, for that indeed was this girl's name (Eileen Cotrell, with her Anglo names hiding while hinting at her Irish-Italian roots) played Amanda with a verve that perhaps veered toward Blanche Dubois on the one hand and Serafina Delle Rose on the other—a juggling act that somehow worked, with her Amanda vying in his eye with Laurette Taylor, and certainly far surpassing Gertrude Lawrence. And this was how the brazen young director decided to have the scene performed in the most modern mode—with his two young actresses switching parts throughout the play, driving the audience and above all Mel mad as he tried to make sense of the senseless.

And so there he was in his own personal confusion as well, dating and deeply in love with the young Jewish girl of his 50s dreams, but unable to fathom his growing fascination for Eileen and his inability even to talk to her. Once the playwrights and actors hooked up at Robbie's, a Telegraph Avenue beer bar, and she looked him in the eye.

"So what's your name after all? " she asked. "I've seen you in the theater a dozen times."

"I'm one of the playwriting students," he muttered, "but I'm really hanging around to see you—or watch you perform."

"Ha!" she said, delighted. "Well what do you think?" she asked. But the brazen director beat him to the punch. "Come on, Eileen, he's obviously head over heels, and the truth is, he thinks you're much better than you could ever be."

"Is that so?" she said. "I'm not so good, right? What do you think?" she asked looking at Mel right in the eye.

"I think you're great," he said, looking back, "even with your crazy director who wants you to play every role at once."

Everyone at the table laughed, and the director responded, "The better to grasp her abundant and varied qualities all at the same time—let there be no doubt."

Mel's special friend Jay whispered to him to be careful "because this girl's a shark and our director friend's a snake."

Mel joined the group for a round of beer. And while he remained withdrawn under the glare of the eyes of the brazen and now alerted director, and under the watchful eyes of Jay and the others, Mel couldn't help telling Eileen that he'd meant what he said.

"One day you'll have to tell me about it," she said, her Irish-green eyes laughing and flirting.

"Yes I will," he answered.

But that was not the day, because she got up and said she had to go. And go she did, kissing this one and that like a grand diva but leaving Robbie's with a certain air of finality.

"A great young woman ripe with all her talents," the director said brazenly "with a great theatrical future before her," he added, "and indeed helped by her mentor's ingenious experiments!"

Almost everyone laughed at the self-compliment but Mel remained silent, thinking of his attraction toward Eileen but all but overwhelmed by his thoughts of Sylvia, one of the last Jewish hopes he was to date and who would throw him over as did the others before and after.

2. Christmas Break

At the same time, of course there were the letters from his mother worrying about his father, his failed hopes for a big job, his finally taking on the job as a cook at an Air Force base, Mel worried about the money he was costing, trying and failing to find work, while yes enjoying his evenings with Sylvia especially in their cinema class, learning so much about film and perhaps too little or too much about each other week by week. But then came the one-month Christmas break, and he returned to L.A. to visit his parents, knowing that Sylvia would follow suit as soon as she was free.

He found that his father was no longer living at home while working at Edwards Airforce base spending long days in lonely exile while he sought to enhance the monthly payment he received from his brother. To Mel, nothing could have been more painful than traveling with his mother on that grim road from the San Fernando valley out to Lancaster in the desert, to see his father doing a job well beneath the level of his talents, living so alone in that alien Anglo Airforce culture.

"My son's in Airforce ROTC," his father bragged to one of the officers.

"No kidding," was the unimpressed reply.

Returning from the base, Mel saw his mother worried and depressed. "This job won't last long," she said, "And the same with the monthly coming in from the restaurant—it won't come in forever. And meanwhile, he keeps on gambling," she added—"yes at the military base too—which is one of the reasons why the job won't last long," she confided when they were ready to park the car.

Sylvia had been working in Berkeley but finally got away and now finally made it to L.A. Aware of her arrival date, he called to see when he could see her, and she said, "Well, Friday, ok?"

"Sure," he said, a little put off because it was only Tuesday. On the designated day, he crossed over the canyon between the Valley and Beverly Hills and over to one of the less chic and lower middle class homes. He sighed with relief when he saw her modest home not so very different from the girls' homes he knew in his Elizabeth, New Jersey hometown. He was also assured by the mezuzah he spotted next to the door. It seemed even more like Elizabeth when it was one of her kid brothers who opened the door, told him Sylvia wasn't ready but he could come in and wait in the finished basement game room. There he sat getting to know the two older brothers and younger sister. Finally Sylvia came in looking as made up and pretty as ever. He felt so fine to be with her, and then to drive around L.A. with her, stopping in at Sherry's bar to catch a set by pianist Pete Jolly, before taking her home. He kissed her in front of her house and told her he wanted her to meet his mom.

"I'd like that. I won't be free much here, seeing friends and relatives, but let's try to get together with your mom next week."

He came by to pick her up and take her to the valley to their modest apartment on Woodman Avenue in North Hollywood, where his mother served up her famous cabbage soup and pot roast, and asked Sylvia where her family came from and how they came to move to L.A. and my goodness, even a modest section of Beverly Hills. Mel balked at the interrogation. But Sylvia defended his mother.

"Mel, she just wants to know what kind of girl you've brought over to her house, and how that girl might hurt her son! It's natural," she said. "Am I right or what?" she appealed to her host.

"Naturally," said the mother, "You know how girls are these days, and how our sons become total idiots when they meet them. Oh, I don't mean you, you can see you're a fine girl made of the right stuff right off. But it never hurts a mother to say something."

"Well, this is probably the best girl you're going to see," said Mel, ogling Sylvia and, his shoes already off, trying to footsy her under the table.

"Mel! Stop that," said Sylvia laughing at him so that Mel felt she loved him, and then somehow felt she was just being friendly while feeling sorry for this Jewish mama's boy.

"What's going on?" said Mel's mother, serving up a famous fancy dessert of hers.

"My god, this is good—I'd gain thirty pounds in a day if you were my mom," Sylvia exclaimed laughing, while Mel hung his head in misery at what he could only understand as a reference to his overweight, unattractive body.

"Well, that's the way it is. Mel's father's always been in the food business and I've been dragged screaming into it to boot, so there's always too much good food around, and that's all there is to it."

"Well," said Sylvia as they prepared to leave, "That was an unforgettable dinner, and it was so wonderful to meet you. Now I know why Mel is such a fine boy, even if he's kinda rough around the edges."

"Well honey, he'll clean up his act someday, with the right girl," said Mel's mother, not making clear if she meant Sylvia or someone else.

"I'm sure he will," said Sylvia. "He's just got to get used to our West Coast ways and he'll be o.k."

"Well, I'm sure there's a lot about the West Coast we can learn from you, so don't you be a stranger now, come back whenever you want."

"Why, thank you so much. I just might do that some time. It was great meeting you."

And so the couple left the house, Mel apologizing all the way back over Coldwater Canyon, and Sylvia telling him not to worry, he had a great mother and he should respect her more.

When they reached her house, she said she'd had a fine time and he suggested they get together as much as they could before returning to Berkeley.

"I'd love to," she said. "But my folks are taking me down to San Diego for a few days, and then it'll be time to fly back up north."

Mel felt a sense of misery set in. He wondered if she wasn't lying to him and giving him the brush. "You're not just saying this so you won't have to see me."

"Mel don't be so silly and insecure. We'll both be back in Berkeley soon and we can take it from there." She let him give her a kiss, Mel wondering if this was a final tryout or a first goodbye.

"Oh, this is just too much, Mel," she whispered to him as he tried to turn the kiss into a total embrace. "Woo! You make me tingle." And then she laughed and got out of the car. "See you in Berkeley, you silly boy," she said.

Mel sensed that it had all been a disaster. He drove around L.A. for hours, hoping for some kind of sexual encounter that would end his virgin misery, but he grew tired, exhausted, his arms drooping over the steering wheel and he just made it home before he was too far gone to continue.

The next weekend, he and his mother drove up to see his father again; and as soon as he got off work, he took them on the road from Lancaster to Las Vegas. They went to the Sahara Hotel and soon were in the casino, where his father went right to the craps table and Mel went with his mother toward the slots.

"You don't worry about me," she said. "You look in on your father, but don't be too obvious. Watch him but don't be hanging all over him. If he starts losing, you should convince him to stop. Luckily, we're going to the show tonight, so he only has an hour. But don't let him fool you. A lot can happen in an hour. Don't let him pawn his watch or do anything crazy. You don't know what he's like in these places—he'll do almost anything."

Off Mel went watching his father on a roll, winning time and again, as the chips piled up. Seeing things were going fine, he drifted off toward a blackjack table and sat down. Before he knew it, he was on a roll of his own, winning well over a hundred, when his mother came by and told him not to leave his father alone for too long.

Reluctantly, he picked up his winnings and left the table knowing he might never be this hot again. But sure enough, when he got to the craps table, he saw that all his father's piles of chips were gone. His father was in a sweat, and Mel watched him lose with each roll of the dice.

"Son," his father said, "Take this watch and see what they'll give you for it."

"Dad come on, it's almost time for the show and you're losing all your money."

"Don't worry about it, my luck was good, and it can be good again. I won't use my credit card so we'll be ok."

"Come on dad," he said. "The show's gonna begin."

"Forget the show—just see what they'll give me for the watch!"

"I can't do it," Mel said. "I promised mom I would stop you. And now you've got to stop."

They were both trying to whisper but their conversation was getting louder, and the croupier was getting embarrassed. "Are you in, sir?" he asked.

"He's out," Mel said, picking up his dad's chips and virtually forcing him to leave in embarrassment.

"I can't believe you did that," his father said. "I've never been so embarrassed."

"Believe me, I hated to do it. But you can't go on like this, Dad," he said, almost in tears and unable to enjoy Lena Horne's songs or even her fading beauty. The next day, they checked out and made their way back to Lancaster, his mother unable to stop herself from talking about her husband's gambling until he pulled the car off the road and shouted, "What do you want me to do, kill myself?" And time and again he smashed his head against the side window.

"Dad!" Mel screamed.

"Don't worry about me," he said. "My life's over, I can't stop and I can't live this down and I might as well die right here in the dessert."

Mel jumped out of the car and opened his father's door. "Come on, Dad, you'll get through this, you'll find something here in California, you'll stop gambling so much and all of this'll be a bad dream." He got him out of the car and maneuvered him into the back seat.

"All I can think about is my brother Al," his father said—"how I cheated my own brother!"

He started crying to himself, and all Mel could say was for him not to worry, Al would be ok and so would he—everything would be fine, he assured, as he took the wheel and began driving back to California, hearing his father sobbing, and then watching in the rear view mirror, how he drifted off to sleep, sleeping all the way back to Lancaster where they dropped him off for his next work week and then headed back to North Hollywood.

3. The Breakdown

Mel drove back to Berkeley, haunted by his father, worried about his relationship with Sylvia and also worried by a phone call he'd received from Larry saying that Kara was pregnant and pressuring marriage. Back in town, he had to move into his new apartment; and once settled in, he called Sylvia only to get Margaret, who told him she was out. He called again and left a second message. On the third call, he finally heard her voice and wooden responses and when he asked when he could see her, she told him she was sorry, but she was involved with someone else. He was speechless and when she too ceased to talk, he hung up the phone. A few days later he ran into her and her new flame, a tall, good-looking Jewish guy, with a wild beard and covered with political buttons.

She called him the next day, apparently to give him pause. "He's a member of SDS," she said, "And I'll be joining soon. You see, you need a more artsy girl, Mel, you're too anti-social and apolitical for someone like me."

He could hardly say a word to this fine girl who would never be his love. Slowly, painfully he put down the phone and hung up.

Only minutes later, he heard from Kara, saying Larry had disappeared, asking if he knew where he was, saying they were supposed to be setting a wedding date and now he'd run off to who knew where. Without dwelling on Sylvia, Mel set out to find his friend, quickly locating him at the apartment of Mike Lerner and his new wife, where he found Larry huddled on the couch, unshaven, shaken and shaking, trembling, staring at the ceiling and the floor or off and away toward some undesignated space beyond.

"He's been like this for three days," Mike said. "Kara keeps calling and we tell her we don't know where he is, but he can't stay like this much longer."

Mel asked Mike to make a pot of coffee and he went in the living room to speak to his friend.

"Larry," he started, what's going on? "

"Nothing," he answered. "Everything's great, I'm the Jewish wonder boy from Burbank and now my life's gone to hell."

"Kara told me she's pregnant," Mel sparred. "It's yours, right?"

"No doubt about that, she's the most honest girl in the world, she is. The perfect girl, but not for the Jewish wonder boy."

Mike brought in the coffee and Mel served Larry a cup, trying to reason with his friend, but already too worked up with his own problems to make much headway with problems that weren't his.

"Listen, Larry, I know Kara's not who you imagined you'd be with. I don't know how you got so involved with her. But maybe it's good, it's your way of getting away from a narrow identity your mom and dad and everyone around you set you up to be. If you're sure you're the father, you've got to make a decision. You don't have to marry her, you can just—"

"I promised I'd marry her. I can't go back on that. And I know I don't love her like I should and it's going to be a disaster."

"Then don't marry her—tell her you just can't, tell her you'll stand behind the baby but you just can't—"

"I have to marry her and I have to make money. I have to forget all I dreamed of doing."

"Larry, don't let yourself be trapped."

"I am trapped, I have to do it, thanks for helping to me realize it."

Mel was astounded. "But I've been telling you just the opposite."

"Yes, in words. But I know what you think and what everyone would think—me most of all. I've got to do it, even if it's the end of my life as I knew it."

With that, and seemingly so little talk or persuasion, Larry got up and called Kara. "Hi honey," he said. "I'm coming home."

Mel drove him over to his apartment with Kara; then he hugged his friend as he got out of the car. Somehow, he sensed that this friendship, like his relationship with Sylvia, was over. With his father, Sylvia and now Larry and Kara, his new California life was collapsing too.

Larry married Kara just days later. And then Mel's own losses and disillusionments hit him square in the chest, knocking the wind out of him and leaving him feeling lost and paralyzed on the Berkeley campus and the Berkeley streets he'd come to love. He fell into a funk that was perhaps as bad as his friend's. Pain and loneliness entered his every pore, a malaise set in such as he read in a novel by Sartre. He tried to study but he couldn't. He turned on his album of Sinatra torch songs and listened day and night, night and day, in the wee small hours of the morning, at almost every hour of every day. He petitioned to reduce his course load to a minimum, went to crisis counseling, but could not rise out of the emptiness he felt.

One day, he received a letter, forwarded by his mother, from Debbie, a high school friend he'd almost fallen in love with and then gnashed his teeth when he fixed her up with his Jewish mentor, Alan Heintz at Dartmouth. And here she was now writing to tell him that she and Alan had decided to get married and how grateful she was to him for having brought them together. Naturally she invited him to the wedding on behalf of them both.

All this left Mel dwelling on his East Coast years in ways he had never done so before. Suddenly, writing plays, meeting Jay, dating Sylvia and all of it had led him to conclude that his life in the east had been a total failure—of him as having positioned himself as out of the game, of him choosing a prosaic life instead of a life of art and literature that had been so much within his early reach. Reading Beckett and Kafka, Mel more and more chose his own way. So taking pen to paper, he congratulated Debbie but indicated that he could not take responsibility for the future of the couple, nor could he consider attending the wedding, since he was locked into studies at Berkeley and now knew that his life path would take him very far away from his previous world. In effect, the east was behind him, high school and Ivy League school behind him and he was in a new life so far from the old one—one in which he would leave behind his public need for popularity and recognition and enter into the deeper levels of art and creation, with the likes of Rimbaud, Kafka, Hesse and Beckett as his guides.

But in fact, he could do nothing to break his downward spiral. Each day he slept later and later, only to rise in time to go for a 35-cent bowl of mushroom barley soup at Robbie's, then for a short walk along and around Telegraph Avenue, and back to his apartment to play his Sinatra and drift off into sleep. Some days he actually made it to campus, heading toward his classes, but usually backing off and returning home. He stopped writing to his parents, stopped trying to contact Larry and virtually left his friend to his own devices, as he sought work before the baby arrived. Mel felt guilty about his friend but felt so disillusioned and defeated there seemed little he could do.

His parents grew alarmed. His father came to visit him, brought him to his hotel room for a few days, but he was so disillusioned by his father he could hardly say a thing, except to promise he'd get more counseling.

"Son, I know it's hard to lose a girlfriend," his father told him. "But it happens to almost all of us, you'll get over this."

Soon his father was on a plane back to L.A. Mel knew the advice he'd been given was right. Thinking clearly, he realized he'd hardly known the girl over whom he so pined. Who was this Sylvia that all the swains (or was it swine?) adored her? Was hers the face that launched a thousand ships? And here his father was advising him without recognizing his own part in what was happening to his son. What could he do but mull over his father's fate, his own lost New Jersey world, the loss of his girl and his best friend in California? Until gradually, so gradually, one day he awoke and began to notice the world around him; and all the things disturbing him seemed to fade just a bit.

Part III. From the Ashes (Spring/Summer 1959)

1. Jack and a New Berkeley World

What broke the downward spiral? Perhaps he had just bottomed out, or had experienced a kind of over-determination. But now he wanted more than mushroom soup. He spoke to some of his teachers, finally won his reduced load petition and dropped classes that were beyond repair, tried to opt out of ROTC (but they wouldn't let him), and only stayed in the classes offered by two brilliant professors, Thomas Parkinson and Fredrick Crews.

Then, attentive to his two professors, he found himself attracted to the short-skirted girls in his class, and also drawn to a male student a bit older than he, who literally leaned over into the laps of the girls seated near him, and rattled his classmates by muttering "Bullshit" to almost everything his brilliant teachers had to say.

Parkinson was a remarkable if rather pretentious professor who simulated an upper class pose to cover his proletarian origins. He took his class through the paces of high modernism, Yeats above all but also Pound, Eliot, and others. Yet all the students knew that he was chummy with the Beats and that he'd made a stir by his defense of Ginsberg's *Howl* at the famous obscenity trial held in downtown San Francisco. Still, for Mel, the crucial moment in Parkinson's class was when his professor held up a copy of Carson McCullers' *Reflections in a Golden Eye*, only to say that such gothic fantasies could never hold a candle to a narrative so true and so penetrating as Anne Frank's *Diary of a Young Girl*.

It was at this point that the gruff male student sitting next to him, whispered in his ear, "This is the first bit of truth that's been said in here all semester."

Mel seemed to wake up, he left the class discussing the matter with the student. They even went for a coffee as they whiled away the hour before their class with Crews.

His name was Jack Delafronde, just out of the army and with funding to take classes at the big u. Still he hated the elitism of the place, the pomposity and pretentiousness of it all. He didn't understand why most of the girls he met were really looking for husbands or at least lovers. Both of them were impressed with Crews' class especially since the teacher seemed no older than they but knew so much. They were struggling over Crews' assignment for a paper on "The Love Song of J. Alfred Prufrock." They went about it in totally different ways, with Jack emulating the very critics he'd read and hated, and Mel attempting an explicative poem of his own, seeking to mimic or restage and explain all.

"This is great stuff," Jack said, reading over Mel's first notes, "but he's gonna hate it—it's not the way things are done here. You can do it or leave it."

Mel persisted and drew a C, with Eliot's women coming and going and talking of Michelangelo, his old man wondering if he should wear his trousers rolled or dare to eat a peach. He grew to believe in his paper, but Jack was right about Crews. He hated it, wrote all over it and despaired, calling it a failed experiment. Then of all things, Crews threw *Pride and Prejudice* at them, insisting on their writing the most academic of papers.

Mel modeled his effort on Empson's *Seven Types of Ambiguity*, showing how that critic's approach led to new insights into irony, comedy, satire and parody, as he teased out the implicit and explicit juxtapositions which he identified as central to the work. Indeed in one long note, which Crews singled out as excellent, he defined the nature of artistic unity. Mel nearly ran over to Jack's apartment to show him the result. "This paper is worthy of a career," wrote Crews.

"That's great," said Jack none too content with his own B.

"Worthy of a career I now know I don't want," said Mel, wondering then what he might do.

Jack lived with a roommate name Van, who shared Mel's passion for theater but as an actor; and soon the roommates invited Mel to leave his breakdown haunt and move in with them. Before he knew it, he'd moved in for the few months remaining before summer break The three became fast buddies cooking Lipton Soup ground-meat beef Stroganoff and big pots of pasta, as they nickeled and dimed a tight food budget and also learned to shop lift for cheese and other sundries. Soon Jack's friend, Bryce Nelson, and his Chinese girlfriend were on the scene; then Van's friend Harold Abrogate, a mad motor cycling Jewish playwright from Brooklyn by way of L.A.'s Boyle Heights. Then Larry came by once in a while to escape Kara; and then his Long Beach friend Bob Kohn, just back from adventures in France, popped by from time to time, until he was just about a regular. Pretty soon there were girls hanging around too, becoming part of a larger group, some of them making passes at one guy or another, leaving Mel in a constant state of expectancy, sexual arousal, and possible post-Sylvia joy.

Van was so uptight; it was hard to imagine him breaking through as an actor. It's true his early forte seemed to be in eighteenth century classics like *She Stoops to Conquer* or Edwardian comedies like *The Importance of Being Ernest*. But once into Ibsen, Strindberg and the line of the modern from Kleist and Büchner to the absurdists, he seemed off his mark. It wasn't clear to Mel why Jack and Van lived together, because they seemed so different. But here they were, with Mel finding his own way into their world.

Jack's closest friend, Bryce Nelson, was quite the young man, knowledgeable about all, with the most marked opinions. In literature, no one was better than Henry Miller, *Tropic of Cancer* topping the list and D.H. Lawrence an impossible sexual romantic. In music, Brahms was a bore, and Puccini somehow rhymed with spaghetti. My god, how the world consumed clichés. Bryce lived on and off with his Chinese girlfriend who did everything for him except set up the appointments for his frequent extracurricular affairs and adventures. Exploiting women was after all proof of your maleness, and Mel believed Bryce needed to confirm his daily.

Harold Abrogate was a burly barrel-chested bear of an Ashkenazi young man (Aleichem's Tevya) with the heart of a poet, and an analytical mind that chimed well in the mix of people who became part of Mel's world. He was always appearing and disappearing you never knew when.

Tall, dark, and wearing like sunglasses, looking like a pimp, Mafioso or French movie star, Bob Kohn rolled into their lives when his friend Larry suggested he try to get to know Mel and his new roommates now that he'd returned from a year of adventures in France, and was ready to start school again. Mel listened with awe as Bob told of his months at sea in the Merchant Marines, his affair with a high-style courtesan, his days as a vineyard worker in rural France, of a whole range of experiences before his return to Berkeley and his efforts to major now in French. He rolled himself a joint and offered me my first toke, showed up, disappeared, showed up again.

As for the women, some of them became regular members of weekly partiers at the apartment on Channing or wherever they could get invites. Bob turned Mel on to pot, as Mel partied his way through the semester, flirting with Vicki, a pock-faced buxom girl, but falling briefly for a Chicana friend of hers from Bakersfield, until Jack warned him:

"Stay away from the *mexicanas*. They usually only go to bed with Mexicans, no matter how much they may complain about their *machismo*. Stick with Vicki—she's your ticket."

Still, Mel just couldn't get himself to join with Vicki, and instead turned toward a slight but pretty Mormon girl named Gennette, who worked as a waitress at the Black Sheep Restaurant and who, apparently liberated from her background, became the girl he saw most and came close to bedding as the semester neared its end.

In those last spring days, through Kara, Mel and Jack connected with a lesbian woman named Pam Gleason, a kind of local Gertrude Stein, and a mutual friend, Betty Lampert, who ended up bedding first with Jack and then visiting and bedding with Jay, who lived in a tiny room, writing his plays and practicing on base. Mel came by Jay's from time to time as he pulled out of his funk, talking to him about art and culture and the new Black nationalism that was sweeping the Black world at decade's end. Jay introduced him to Reynolds Jailer and a few other brothers committed to the new ethos, though Jay remained ironically distant, giving his life to art, and soon performing his base for money and joy at La Valle's pizzeria on the northside. Mel mainly hung out with his white friends, but more and more he leaned toward Jay, Jailer and those who called whites devils. They even took him to see Malcolm X, who, still with Elijah Mohammed, cursed the white man and fomented rebellion, Mel cheering along with the rapt audience.

It was in this new life, that Mel got in the habit of rising early and hammering out some pages of prose, writing finally the best story he'd yet produced, a short one about his relationship with his sister, which just hummed with their ambivalent dialog and which he called then, "Valentine's Day 1947." He was on a new high, sensing that life was opening for him. But, lacking money or work to sustain him in Berkeley for the summer, he made ready to return to L.A., saying goodbye to his friends and to Genette, telling them he'd be back in the fall.

2. L.A. Again

Having pulled out of his depression, Mel was almost pulled back in that summer when his father bit the bullet and bought the job he could no longer find by purchasing a thriving coffee shop in downtown L.A.'s Occidental Life Insurance Building. Sometimes he went in at six with his dad. Other times, he took the bus downtown with his mother. Always it was traffic jam on traffic jam, and then the misery of the long workday, waiting on the counter, dealing with take outs, cleaning things up and doing all there was to do. His father was intent on making the coffee shop work, with its captive clientele in the building and those he could lure in by his street signs and word-of-mouth. The best of it was going down to the Central Market each morning to buy the produce for the day, finding the specials—cantaloupes, watermelons, mangoes— all kinds of things that would perk up sales and spread the word that this coffee shop was special. But midsummer came and with it the realization that his father had been conned, that Occidental and its teeming shifts of workers were abandoning the building that August and that the previous owner and the Occidental staff had known this but had said nothing about it. Soon the workers were moving and the business declined until there were no lines at breakfast or lunchtime, and the place was going bust.

A new grey cloud overcame his father and Mel felt it as well. It went along, however, in a desperate rise in his youthful sexual desires and his need to satisfy them. In the evenings after long days at work, he would cruise L.A. with an Elizabeth friend Dickie Arnold, who was now ensconced selling used cars in Culver City and who always picked different cars for his summer night forays with Mel trying to pick up girls on Sunset or Hollywood Boulevard. One evening they followed two crazy girls as they chased after Ricky Nelson down a narrow Hollywood Street. "Ricky, Ricky!" they screamed.

"Hey girls, I'm Dickie," he said pulling alongside the girls. "Put up or shut up," said one, and Dickie lowered his pants to show what he had. The girls oohed and ah-ed and then went tearing off down the street.

On another night, they drove around with Dickie's friend Joe and actually corralled a nurse at a bus stop, picking her up and bringing her to her apartment, where Dickie and Joe took turns on her as she gasped and sucked until the two young men were all spent.

"Is that all you got?" said the nurse. Dickie tried again without success. "And what about this guy sitting in the corner?" the hungry nurse asked Dickie.

"Come on, Mel," Dickie urged, but Mel just couldn't get himself to go. He didn't want this to be his first experience.

Somehow, he resisted the taunts of Dickie, Joe, and the crazed nurse, standing his ground until they left the apartment.

"Jesus, you're no fun," said Dickie.

"Maybe he likes boys," Al sneered.

Mel just remained silent until they got to his car, where he buzzed off without saying a word, to get some sleep before going to the dying coffee shop early in the morning.

It was in those fading August days that Mel felt himself grow wild about a beautiful office worker who continued coming into the shop even as the business fell to ruin. It seemed Occidental was dis-occupying floor by floor and they hadn't reached hers yet. So each day she would show up and sit at the counter, waiting for Mel to take her order. Somehow, she seemed totally different from the other women, dressing with ever such good taste, laughing more lightly than the others, speaking in a more precise, educated way, as if she were going to a fine eastern college like the ones that he had known just a year before.

Mel just couldn't figure her out, and there was hardly time to say anything at the counter because she hardly ever came in alone and her friends seemed to think that their job was to protect her from poor jerks like him. However, as the business slackened off, she'd endeared herself to Mel by commenting on the situation.

"I feel so bad about what's happened here," she said "especially when your boss has worked so hard to make this place the best choice you could have for lunch in downtown LA." And when she realized Mel's boss was his father, she was especially kind and sympathetic. "How rotten," she told him, "and they told him nothing when they sold him the place?"

This conversation led to others and Mel realized what he'd already sensed—that she was no regular Occidental secretary, but rather, like him, a college student with a summer job in L.A. As it turned out, she was a Jewish girl from Scarsdale, New York, and just in L.A. for a few more weeks. Mel was discouraged by all this and knew she was just too good-looking for him anyway, but he couldn't help trying; so he asked her if she was free Friday evening and might wish to go out with him.

"Oh," she said, "sure. I'm staying with my uncle near UCLA in the Belair section of West LA. It's gated," she added "— super-exclusive. But I'll tell them you're coming so they'll call me when you get there. I should be ready by eight."

She wrote out the address for him and went back to work, while he looked miserably at the paper, knowing beforehand that he was going where angels feared to tread.

He didn't see her that Friday, but that evening, he came home early, shaved, showered, put on the best of his meager wardrobe and drove over Coldwater Canyon, to Sunset Boulevard, and then west to the area indicated. Arriving at the gate, he handed over his ID, heard the call made and received the ok to enter. The house of course was a mansion with two sports cars parked in the driveway. Mel felt the immediate urge to leave, or, at least, to seek the back door. But he got a grip on himself, parked on the sidewalk adjacent to the driveway—not in front of the walkway, but in front of an expanse of lawn—and made his way not up the walkway, but the driveway itself, arriving at the front door after all, ringing the bell and waiting until he heard a latch turn and she let him in.

She was dressed in the tightest pants you could imagine, with a satin lavender blouse, large, provocative hoop earrings, and the highest of heels a woman could wear. Her makeup accentuated her high cheek bones, her deep eyes— he found her too dazzling to think of approaching. She tried to make him at home, offered him a glass of wine, which he took trembling and fearful that he'd spill it on the vast white rug, the white upholstery and maybe her clothes, if not his. He understood they were not leaving the house until her uncle met the young man who had dared to ask her out. And sure enough, uncle appeared—not the older man he'd imagined but a young man in his mid-thirties, clearly a swinging bachelor of his time and place, dressed to kill and on his way out for the evening.

"Hi," he said, pouring himself a drink, and making small talk. It turned out he was a Hollywood writer with some impressive film credits. "I graduated from the film program at UCLA, and then it was a hop, skip and a jump into the industry," he said.

As a lover of Beckett and Kaka, Mel refused to be impressed. But he did let on he hoped to be a writer, and uncle and niece encouraged him to consider the industry.

"Let's make a date for me to show you around the studios," said the uncle. "Then maybe you can tell if this is for you. It certainly is for me." And with that, he surprised Mel by excusing himself and making toward the door. "I don't know what you two are going to do, but I've got a date in twenty minutes." And out the door he went, leaving the two to their own devices, as he revved his sportscar motor and went flying on his way.

"Well," she said, "that's that." And pouring him another drink of wine, she asked him where he thought of taking her. He mentioned one of his standby L.A. jazz clubs, but she said, "Why don't we stay here? We have the house to ourselves and we're both leaving back to school soon, so this might be the only chance we have to get to know each other."

She put on some Miles, and they sat and talked of their lives, this or that and whatever. According to his understanding of things, no woman would be dressed as she was and would invite him to stay if she didn't intend some intimacy or sexual contact as part of the evening's activity. But he also knew he had to bide his time, wait until she was ready, sent him a signal of some kind. He couldn't get himself to be interested in what she said, in her life in Scarsdale, her first boyfriends and loves, because she would be gone in a few days, perhaps even before they had a chance to see each other again. So what could it matter? Why waste his life energy unless indeed he intended to write about their meeting some day? He knew he was poor in spirit, but though lifted by recent friendships and encounters, he still suffered the wounds of Sylvia's rejection and all that had happened to him earlier in the year. So he listened to her and then told his own stories of love and life in New Jersey, New York and Dartmouth, before leaving the east coast just two years before. He readily accepted every glass of wine she offered because he knew that might turn his fantasies to reality. But he was sober enough to note that even though she matched him in drinks, she seemed to be holding on to herself a little better than he.

Gradually he felt himself staring more and more into her eyes, watching her wonderful mouth, seeking to position his body next to her ever-slouching form. On and on they talked, while his fantasy of making love to this beautiful girl grew by leaps and bounds. Suddenly, she was in his arms, indeed draped over him as he felt the excitement within him grow and his caresses turned from affection to passion. And then, when she seemed to him so ready for further advances, he suddenly felt her inert, heavy against his body, and he realized that she had completely collapsed in his arms. She even began to snore slightly, and it was clear that nothing would wake her soon. He felt his disappointment ever so keenly, felt the loss of a possible life opportunity. Surely the evening could not end like this. Surely she would wake up soon. But the minutes and time itself went by, and it became clear that there was no way she would come back to this world for some hours.

"Nothing to be done," he quoted Hamm talking to Clov as *Endgame* began. He extricated his body from hers, propped a cushion under her head, covered her lightly with a comforter ready at hand, retrieved his glasses and made his way to the front door, opening it and then closing it behind him as he made his way to his car, put the key in the ignition and drove off, as his great dream and adventure came to a dismal conclusion.

Part IV. New Urban Encounters (1959-60)

1. Starting Life in the City

Summer break almost over, his dream girl gone back east, his father's business all but dead, it was getting time to return to Berkeley. But just as he was getting set, he received his grades from the spring semester, which, lower than usual because of his winter breakdown indicated B's in English, a C in French and an F in Airforce ROTC. In effect, he would have to take ROTC all over again. And that he could not do. He had left Dartmouth and now he was being forced out of a school he loved where he'd even managed to develop friendships and structure a future for himself.

"Nothing to be done," he quoted Beckett again. Berkeley without ROTC and repeating ROTC were not options. He had to transfer as soon as possible to San Francisco State College, further down the social ladder, but with the redeeming attraction of a budding creative writing program of which he might become part. He called Admissions and explained his situation. He was now a state resident, so the price wouldn't be too high, and yes, they would let him in at this late date. So he enrolled by mail and made his way north to confirm it all and begin the process of moving to San Francisco.

On arrival his friends urged him to stay in Berkeley and commute. But his car wasn't for that, and it just wasn't going to work out because now he had to find a job. Forlorn as could be, he crossed the bridge and began his big search for an apartment, eager at the same time to live the life of the city. But the only decent and reasonably priced place he could find for himself was in the Sunset District, far from the core urban action and far from the bridge that would quickly take him back to his Berkeley world.

The apartment was a pristine, white studio you reached through a door inside the garage, past the washer and dryer. It was all so neat and all too isolating for a young man needing some kind of sociability to match his need for privacy. It was some $45 a month, which fit his budget, even though he would end up spending much on gas and transportation just to be part of the life of the city.

It was pretty close to San Francisco State, however—only some fifteen minutes away, and near the ocean too, where he could go for a walk on weekends. The neighborhood was all too suburban and depressed him on his return to isolation each day. The San Francisco State campus also depressed him, with its chintzy buildings and landscape as signs of his decline down the academic and social ladder. All this changed with certain of his professors—above all, that first semester, Walter Van Tilburg Clark, the writer of *The Ox-Bow Incident*, an ex-gym teacher who each day wore a grey sweatshirt to class and who each day brilliantly dissected another short story, showing how the story was made and what a story was. There were other courses he took that first semester—a writing class with Mark Harris, best known for his baseball novel, *Bang the Drum Slowly*, and a class on Faulkner with Ruth Witt-Diamont, who complained how Harris had appropriated her name for the pitcher Witt Diamond in another of his novels. Absorbing Faulkner, he felt himself trapped by his style and wondered if he could both read the fascinating works and still retain his own voice. But he was game, he felt, for whatever came his way.

2. The Waitress and the Writer

One day on campus, he was shocked to see Gennette, who told him she had also transferred from Berkeley. Had she moved there to be with him? Perhaps his isolation was about to be broken. He drove her over to see his apartment, they even kissed and petted a bit on his bed, testing the water for the future, perhaps. But neither wished to move further that afternoon, and he drove her home, saying he had to work on a paper and a new story he was writing, and he was also looking for a job, but he'd call her when he was more settled in.

Quickly he found a job in the shipping department of a downtown clothier, Arnelle of California. The first day his boss asked him to put a bolt of cloth in his green Ford station wagon, parked outside, for a delivery he had to make. Once on the sidewalk, he spotted a car fitting the description given, lifted the rear door, placed the bolt inside, and then returned to his worksite. A little later, he received a call from the boss and went upstairs.

"Where the hell's the bolt?" the boss asked. "I put it in the station wagon," he answered.

"Well it's not there."

"But I put it there."

"Did you lock the door?"

"I didn't have the key."

"For Christ's sakes, and you call yourself Jewish? You little schmuck! You can't leave a car open on Sutter Street."

"But you left the door open."

"You mean you found the door open?"

"Yes," he said, eyeing him sharply.

"You're saying it's my fault, you fucking prick?"

"I didn't say that," Mel answered.

Luckily he wasn't fired and he soon found himself delivering things all around the city, and mainly the sweatshops in every neighborhood that housed them. The key one was right next to that Beat holdover, The Wine Cellar, where he went to hear Pony Poindexter, King Pleasure, and others. There several women worked in the worst conditions, as the musicians played on and their public downed their drinks. Oh the great bohemian life.

Meanwhile, he worked under a Mexican supervisor, George Silver. "I used to be Jorge Silva," he told Mel. "But they told me I should change my name so it would sound Jewish, 'cause Jews know how to make it—like you," he added. "Pretty soon you'll be my boss." Anticipating the worst, Silver gave Mel the worst jobs. And sure enough, right next door to the Wine Cellar, Mel entered to find a group of Chinese women sewing with raw light bulbs blaring, leaving his bolts and making a quick retreat back to his car and on to his next miserable spot. He felt shame for the lower depths of Arnelle and for the Beat pretensions as well.

At the same time, each day, Mel returned home to finish his paper on Faulkner's "That Evening Sun" and its relation to the same author's *Sound and the Fury*. And meantime too, he worked on a new and heart-wrenching story, the story of his father, in a long short story or novella that haunted him day and night.

He finally drafted the paper for Walter Van Tilburg Clark, and realized he could expand it, as the basis for an overall examination of discrepancy in Faulkner's work for Witt-Diamont, focusing on *The Sound and the Fury* but also *Absalom, Absalom!*, and all works related to the Compson family. In the meantime, he completed the story of his father's gambling disgrace in Elizabeth, a story he called "One Way to California." It was painful and cathartic to write and rewrite this story, drawing on Fitzgerald, Arthur Miller and even Dreiser's *Sister Carrie*, to get at the deeper truths he had to narrate. Immediately he submitted his papers and his story.

Van Tilburg Clark was impressed, Witt-Diamont very pleased, with the papers; and Irving Halperin said, the story of his father was "great—it's really perfect in its way, you shouldn't change a thing. You should send it off."

Thrilled as he was by all this, he decided he couldn't send the story anywhere because his parents and his family were alive. Instead, he simply focused on re-doing "The Hunger Artist" to reduce its chaos and make a smaller but more ordered play. Days and nights went by, and he couldn't seem to finish the manuscript. When he finally did, he sent it to Marvin Rosenberg, thanking him for all he taught. Professsor Rosenberg wrote back saying the play worked now and urging him to submit it for contest in story adaptation held by a theatre group in Menlo Park near Stanford. He did so and was deep into the semester; and it was only then that he tried to contact Genette, only to find that she'd changed phones and indeed had dropped out of school.

So went his possible new love, and on he went alone, wondering what had happened to her, but working at his job and his classes, having virtually no social life and no campus life, as time rolled by.

3. Jay, Lee, and the Women

It's so hard for him to recall the days after that, the year and a half before the summer he met Marlena and the life of his mid-twenties began. He can remember that in the fall or winter, he walked through San Francisco's Black Filmore District with Jay, passing every miserable dive and slum apartment on their way, eating some rich soul food, and having just the best and maybe only significant time with him since he'd moved out of Berkeley. Jay said he didn't have time to come to San Francisco too often, but he insisted on hooking Mel up with a friend or acquaintance of his, named Lee Smith.

"Lee hangs at the Wine Cellar, he can hook you up with all the ladies in the Bay area," Jay told him. "Because it looks like you could use a little leg."

Lee lived in the Filmore, but they indeed caught up with him at the Wine Cellar, Jay telling Lee to take care of his friend, as he got set to cross the bridge with another friend of his. Lee was never very talkative, and sometimes Mel had a sense that he might be a pimp more than a ladies' man. but he was always introducing Mel to different people—mainly white girls who rather clearly had come looking for cool Black men but might in a pinch end up with a would-be Jewish writer. One night Mel found himself falling for a vivacious girl who came in with two white boys, both of them ever so chummy with her. They asked to sit at his table, and sure enough, they were all laughing and joking with him, until the girl went for the bathroom, and the other two discouraged him about her, telling him she was basically a lesbian friend waiting for one of her girlfriends to come by.

"My god," Mel said, his dream shattered, though he still couldn't hide his attraction. (Was this a key moment on the road to Marlena?) Then Lee came in and took him aside, telling him he needed a favor, that Mel should stop messing around with that lesbian bitch and take over for him hosting a pretty homely girl that had come into town to meet him when he had more precious coals on the fire. Reluctantly Mel eased off and let Lee lead him to his table, where, after introductions, Lee got up saying he'd be back soon, leaving them never to return.

As the girl got wise to the ruse, she was resentful and almost in tears. But a few drinks began to change that, and before you knew it, Mel had convinced her she was too drunk to drive home and that she should just stay and enjoy the evening with him. As he drank, he realized how desperately horny and alone he was. The girl was far from attractive, but he calculated, that might make it easier for him to manipulate her as Lee or others might do. Sure enough, he finally had her in his car, racing all the way out along the ocean road that led ultimately to his boudoir apartment. There, wearing a pair of his pajamas, she began to mount him and rubbing her clitoris against his erect penis, riding him externally with near desperation until she came dispersing her pent-up energy. She was so happy, she was thrilled. She apologized for not having coitus with him, promised she would the next time. But Mel had already decided there'd be no next time. She made eggs for the two of them, polished off the last of his coffee, milk and juice and then had him take her back to her car so she could go over to her folks' house as she tended to do after church on Sundays.

Mel decided Lee was not his ticket and he tried to stay away from the Wine Cellar. But soon after, Jay called him to ask if they could meet at a supper club where one of his military buddies was giving a kind of one-night stand maybe as an audition for future gigs. His name was Donald Washington, a good looking guy wearing a gorgeous tuck as he warbled torch songs much in the style of Billy Eckstein, Billy Daniels, Herb Jeffries or Al Hibler. Leaving the place with Donald, they headed toward an after-hours jazz club, where the two African American vets rehearsed for him all their military high jinx; then he and Jay took Donald to the Trailways station where he boarded the bus to his next gig in Eugene Oregon. Mel and Jay sadly agreed Donald wasn't going to make it as a singer and wondered what he might next do with his life. Mel offered Jay a ride home and they just hung out that day in Jay's tiny, bathroom-less apartment, filled with books and a small writing table, with Jay's working notebook. Mel spent hours reading Jay's latest play efforts—struck especially by one he was trying to do on the Conquest of Mexico. They talked about Jay's upbringing in New Mexico, his period as a catcher in the Mexican leagues going town to town—neither of them knowing how things Mexican and Latin American would affect the rest of their lives.

They talked about Richard Wright, James Baldwin, and Ralph Ellison, about Sartre, Camus, Genet and others. Jay played bass for him, showed him a sketch that captured his sensitivity and physical beauty, so that Mel had to question who had executed the sketch. "Betty," Jay answered. "Betty Lampert." She drives over sometimes, you know, and then drives me and my bass over to LaValle's where she draws folks while me and the piano player make our music."

That afternoon, though, he invited Mel to go with him to Oakland to meet a very special girl he knew. Alice was her name, and he had also met her at LaValle's, right in front of Betty for all Mel knew, and Mel went with him to her house because she'd just bought the latest album by Coltrane. Mel was immediately taken with her, as Jay apparently wanted him to be, and the three talked on and on analyzing the new Coltrane sound—the extended, seemingly endless solos, the tricks, the sound, the complete expression of the sax as ego.

"I don't know if he's the beginning or end of jazz," Jay said.

"He's surely a genius," Alice interjected.

"Yes," Jay agreed, "but maybe jazz is best with severe limits like on the old 78s or 45s where you had to do it all, create or die, on one or two choruses."

The argument went back and forth, until he had to get ready for LaValle's. Alice said she'd try to join them, but it just didn't happen, and Mel never saw her again.

4. Jay in L.A. and Laura Rachel Israel in Berkeley

In the days before and after Christmas, Arnelle gave him some days off, and this time he hooked up with Jay in L.A. (he had come down to San Pedro to visit his father). Mel drove over to the coast to pick him up and take him over to his North Hollywood home to meet his mom and dad, who were perhaps overly polite. Later that evening, Mel ended up as the only white boy at an almost all black party in almost all Black Compton. How Jay knew about it was never clear, but Jay was like that—living in isolation and knowing about everything.

Then it was back to the Bay area, back to see his Berkeley friends, to see where they were at, staying a few days before classes and work started. One night he went to the Cinema Guild to see one of the great classic films Pauline Kael was always programming for the theater; and somehow in the lobby, he started talking to a pretty gypsy-like Jewish girl, Laura Rachel Israel. After the film they went for coffee talking about their young lives and dreams. He walked her home and they agreed to have dinner two days down the road. He had never dated any girl Jewish like her. She was on a year's leave to develop her musicianship and study composition, she told him, from Sarah Lawrence University, where she had been studying with Miriam Rukeyser, poet, activist and feminist, long before so many other famous women. She was a bohemian girl, a lover of classical music and literature, a cellist, a poet, a writer. She told him she needed to decide if her road would be literature or music.

"Why can't you do both?" he asked.

And she explained to him earnestly that each was a discipline that required constant practice. Trying to do both was almost impossible. So the gypsy bohemian girl was also a perfectionist, always careful not to take on more than she should—which perhaps helps explains what happened. In the days which followed, he read her fiction, listened to her records, her recorded rehearsal exercises. They had started holding hands at movies, at chamber concerts that were constantly taking place in Berkeley. She invited him to a three-night series of recitals of Bartok's quartets by a major group, and he listened ecstatic, attempting to grasp the most difficult and powerful pieces, fully entering into a music that seemed as pained and dissonant as the times, almost forgetting Sylvia and falling in love with this truly right kind of girl for the emerging him he was becoming. She supposedly had a boyfriend, David, whose name (the same name Mel had designated for his child-self, after the Biblical shepherd boy and adulterer, but also for D.H. Lawrence). And wasn't Sarah Lawrence a college named for the mother of the reactionary proletarian novelist, his favorite British writer for many years? In any event he hated this rival David who was her excuse for not making love with him, for leaving him now so old and still a virgin. He wept in frustration, looking for any gesture that suggested she might be now loving him a little bit even as she tried to retain her fidelity to David. And then, some wine, some talk in her apartment, she reading from her own writing, he reading some of his, with each filled with wonder at the other—before they knew it, they were undressed and in bed, he for the first time, marveling as she peeled off her black leotard stockings, as she took off her bra and as they embraced body to body, and then began the ritual meeting, as he ever slowly achieved his erection and entered her, however tentatively, timidly, ineptly, and all very much too quickly, finally orgasming, leaving her on the shore, undoubtedly disappointed with his lovemaking and yes, with him.

"It's always so wonderful to make love, it brings people so close," she said, vaguely, flatly, without reference to any love or deep feeling she might feel toward him. Soon he got dressed sensing she was easing him out the door, wondering if she would want to see him again.

"I'm sorry," he said, leaving, his head still filled with Bartok's painful dissonances and her sweet breathing. "It'll be better next time, I promise," he said, wondering if she would let there be a next time.

And sure enough when he called her the next day, she sounded tentative and distant. And when he pressed her, she told him she liked him very much and had gotten carried away, but her true love was David and she should not betray him again.

"Please," he pleaded, "don't call this off when we're just getting started. This could be a beautiful relationship."

"Yes," she agreed, they had much in common, she liked him very much, she repeated almost wearily. But she had to devote more time to her music and of course David was waiting, and indeed was coming to visit her, and he had to understand that she couldn't even see him on a friendly basis without risking her core relationship, that she was sure he would make a wonderful mate for another girl, but she was already spoken for. And he kept wondering if this were a direct response to his inept lovemaking, his bald head, his smallness of size, whatever. And she no longer returning his calls and he lost without her, lost back in his San Francisco routine. He even dreamed of kidnapping her, dreamed of coming to her apartment with rope and pillowcases, to tie her up to take her with him down the road, while he finally could say what was in his heart and win back the wonderful girl he had never truly had, and as he gave up on his plot, he realized, that he never would see her again in this life.

5. Parkinson, Harold, Runter, Bob and Crazy Bay Area Days

Much had changed even in the few months he'd been going to San Francisco State. Personal violence was all around, somehow anticipating the political turn that was about to burst forward in Berkeley and the country. SDS was already very active; people were buzzing about a second wave of McCarthyism; protests were underway about the imminent execution of Caryl Chessman. Gradually things converged on Mel's own little world. His Yeats professor Thomas Parkinson was sitting in his office with a graduate teaching assistant when another student, enraged against the professor's radical views, entered the office and shot both men, killing the assistant and leaving Parkinson broken and face-damaged for life. Real life was indeed more unbelievable than literature.

Only some days later Mel heard that, with tightened campus security, Harold Abrogate was arrested and expelled for riding his motorcycle through the ground floor of Bancroft library—roaring down one ramp, then blazing his way throughout the entire reading room and out the other side. Caryl Chessman was executed on Death Roy, May 2, 1960; just days later, Mel watched on television as protestors against the House Un-American Committee, including several members of SDS (maybe including Sylvia Lachter's boyfriend and maybe Sylvia too) were hosed down the stairs of the Federal Building.

Mel visited Jack only to find Harold and Bob there too, with Bob embittered and enraged because his French teacher, good old Arthur Runter, had given him an F for the second time, thereby preventing Bob from graduating. Bob was deep into a funk; he had tried talking to Runter, a gloomy and apparently bitter Jewish professor from New York who refused to see him saying he would not risk his objectivity. Why couldn't this man spare him and let him get on with his life? Bob's funk turned into a depression edging toward desperation, Mel thought. He was probably on pills; something had snapped in him. Recently expelled, Harold identified fully with Bob, and let loose a tirade about Berkeley's upwardly mobile New York Jewish professors who specialized in the great Anglo or French traditions and had it in for the next generation of their fellow tribe members who could show them up as uppity and maybe outshine their own compromised and falsified lives. All four jumped into Harold's car and Jack took the wheel driving Bob around town as Harold laid out his plan to terrorize this vicious Jew-hating Jewish professor known for his moral and morose rigidity.

"He probably hasn't fucked in years, and he's probably hot for your beautiful body," said Jack to Bob.

Harold had them stop the car and pulled out a broom from his car trunk. As darkness fell, Harold urged Jack to drive onto campus.

"Take me past his office," Harold insisted, and Jack obliged, who knows why. He spotted someone leaving Dwinelle Hall, the building where Runter had his office and where Parkinson had been shot.

"Go after him," Harold urged. And as Jack pulled up, Harold stuck the broom handle through his open window and fired on the walking figure, "Bang! Bang!" Harold shouted as his probably innocent targ, raced for the bushes running like Bannister and Landy combined.

"Bang!" Harold shouted again, and then Bob broke into tears. "The bastard," he muttered.

"Harold, you're crazy," Mel said. "After what happened to Parkinson, the cops would arrest you even for waving a soggy mop. ... We could all've been hauled in.

"Why couldn't he give me a D and let me pass?" Bob asked, completely ignoring Mel's comment.

The next Saturday, as a kind of cure for Bob's deep woes, Harold, Jack, and Mel lured him into a little trip through the Napa Valley. Off they went, with Harold playing guitar in the backseat, seconded by Mel singing away, with Jack driving and Bob at his side, wearing sunglasses and almost out of it from the start as they went down one road and then another, flitting from winery to winery, and then taking the deep cavern tour at Berringer wines.

"Man, your funk can't be sunk as dark and deep as this dump," chimed Harold, making his bid for poet laureate. "So let's get you as drunk as a skunk, you lunks!"

They tasted and bought too much, and almost went off the road more than once as they raced through the countryside and over to Bodega Bay for a view and snacks before heading home. On the way back, Bob got sick and began vomiting out the window. As if out of sympathy, Abrogate and Mel began to vomit along with him as they careened their way down the highway, barfing and laughing, with Jack the only one remaining sober enough to get them home without a scratch.

6. Goodbye to Jack

As the spring deepened, Jack made it clear he was going to Paris to study, so he and Van gave up their apartment and came over to the city to live with Mel before the Parisian adventure began. Mel had moved out of his Sunset home and joined his friends in renting a dark, miserable Medical Center area apartment near Golden Gate Park. Bob came by once in a while and even Harold dropped by and announced that, booted out of UC, he too had enrolled in playwrighting classes at San Francisco State. It seemed that Bob on the other hand had confronted the UC administration about his Runter problem and succeeded in convincing them to get around Runter by taking another course that would lead to his graduation. The course was a pushover, and Bob was proud of his hutzpah and thrilled by his success, buzzing off to who knew where, so they hardly saw him. All the while, Jack, Van and Mel were all working like mad inside and outside of school, with Mel and Van taking on part-time jobs, with Harold working to pay for his new apartment, and with Jack working the most to save money for his year abroad.

Of course, too, some things happened that maybe were too much. The young apartment mates grew gradually aware of a middle-aged woman living on the floor below them. She was a heavy drinker and smoker and hated to do her drinking or smoking alone, so she was always inviting young medical students over, flirting with them and even offering herself to them if they'd help her with the rent, the heat, the cigarettes, and booze. One night she knocked on the roommates' door desperate for drinks, getting a couple of beers sprawling over a couch, as if she planned to stay the night, and finally showing them the strange problem she had with the left hand middle finger which curved up as if she were giving them the bird.

"Just an accident," she said, "But you could take it as an invitation," she said, trying to provoke them, even as they all but pushed her out of the apartment.

One night things the roommates heard a ruckus and even screams from her apartment, and rushed down to find her screaming and throwing things at two young men, one zipping up his pants, the other struggling to get his shirt on, both of them trying to get out the door just as the roommates came in.

"Get out of here, you cheap mother fuckers," she shrieked. "A promise is a promise and you've had your last fuck party with me!" she shouted after them, but then collapsed on the couch and started to cry.

"Those bastards promised to help me with the rent!" she shrieked. She kept on crying fiercely as Van gave her a cigarette, trying to call her down. "They just took me for peanuts and when I asked for my money, they started punching at me." She cried for a while but then started to revive, offering them drinks they declined to drink, and then offering herself to them as she'd apparently done to her previous visitors, but the roommates made for the door. "Come on," she called after them, "it's still early and there's still some booze left."

They didn't hear from her for some days, but then one night she ran into Jim and Mel as they were walking up the stairs. "You guys ready to party tonight?" she asked, clearly drunk and ready for another adventure. When they declined, she got abusive with threats and warnings. And the next day the landlord came by to tell the roommates that she had complained about their noisy, abusive ways. "I'm not blaming you," he said. "But I'll tell you what I told her. I'm tired of the bullshit and it's time you all moved out."

Jack was getting ready to leave on his European trip, and Mel and Van decided it was time to look for another place. They found it in Noe Valley, the other side of Market Street from the Castro District—a neat little first floor apartment with room for two or three, just right for the two of them and of course Jack in his last days. Soon they moved out, choosing a day when the crazy neighbor wasn't around, and settling in to their new place.

Once in, Jack took Mel with him to visit his older brother Ron who was living in his gay bachelor's pad in North Beach. Mel marveled at the view and elegance even as he noted how hostile Jack was to his brother because of his flippant and superior manner, as if being gay made him somehow better, and that he had a right to be irresponsible in ways Jack never could.

Jack was always the cynical and ruthless commentator, a fine writer in the tight Hemingway mold, who kept trying to tell Mel he had to live his life with greater unbending courage, not giving in or being taken in by so much. "U.S. life's leaving me soft," he told Mel. "You need to get out too," Jack added, though they never got out together.

"Jack's really gifted," Mel thought, reading his friend's breathless story about a Mexican woman moving on bleeding hands and knees toward the image of Guadalupe in a rural church. "But he seems burdened by his sense of obligation to live up to an image others have of him—"l'enfer c'est autres," he intoned, wondering if Jack could survive as a writer with all this on him. For all his talk, he simply wasn't ruthless or amoral like his friend Bryce Nelson. And confronted with his brother's attitudes, he was bitter and angry. Ostensibly they'd come there so Jack could say goodbye, but also get some tips from his brother who'd lived in Paris for two years.

Given his French surname, Ron had a special affinity toward the country and language; but unimpeded by any sense of responsibility, and with his heightened sense of sociability, Ron had easily mastered the language and taken Parisian culture and style to heart. Yet when Jack asked for recommendations, all he seemed to get was a list of gay bars and gay friends. He knew his brother knew more than this but was teasing him on purpose to see if he could set him off. Sure enough, he'd prepared them a beautiful meal, choosing a wine he clearly thought more suitable than the obvious student cheapo they'd brought him. And just when dinner was winding down with his outrageous suggestions and comments, the door rang, and in came Ron's other guest, a very gay young man who carried a little duffle bag making it perfectly clear that he'd come over for more than dinner and brother-meeting. As the sun set, they all went out on the terrace to look at the stars on this clear San Francisco night.

Ron and his friend then moved to the couch while the visitors finished up their wine on the balcony. When they came in the two young men were giggling, hugging and even kissing on the couch.

"Thanks a lot, Ron," Jack said, grabbing his coat and Mel's and heading toward the door.

"Have a great trip," called Ron from the couch.

"Yeah," Jack said. "With your great advice, how can I fail?"

The next day, Mel drove Jack to the airport. "Gonna miss you much, my friend," Mel said. "You saved my life in Berkeley and even here in the city, and now you'll be gone for a year. You'll probably come back a married man," he joshed.

"I'll probably come back with the clap," Jack said, "Take care of yourself and look out for our crazy friends and the insane girls you always fall for."

Mel knew that Jack had virtually rescued him in his breakdown. He wondered what their future would bring.

Part V. Rooming, Lusting, and Stage-Struck (1960-61)

1. Van, Joanie and Others

Now on their own, Mel and Van settled into their placid, distant relationship that never seemed to get much closer. Van was so formal and escaped into acting; he couldn't relate to Mel's playwriting efforts, and Mel found his acting superficial and only good for light drawing room comedy—indeed, the whole gamut of British comedy from *She Stoops to Conquer* to Noel Coward. Mel was engrossed in his studies of British Renaissance drama, in absurd theatre, and modern French literature, as well as his work for Arnelle and his own writing. He took one literature and writing class after another, peppered with required courses in Physical Ed., choosing archery, bowling, and boating. When he had the money, he went to see the Actor's Workshop productions, as well as the few jazz venues the Bay area offered. Once in a while he'd fall for a girl in one of his classes. First there was the student actress from the Workshop—she who played a prostitute in *The Balcony*, and a maid in a revival of Ben Jonson's *Alchemist*. Then it was a striking Irish redhead in one of his creative writing classes, who let him visit her in her Richmond home in a converted firehouse, smoked a joint with him, but then made it clear they would not become lovers.

Soon Van had a girlfriend, Joanie, who frequently stayed with him at the house on Ort Street. The house was crazy in its shotgun setup, with a front parlor, a living room, dining room and kitchen straight in a row, a tiny room off the kitchen and no other completely private bedroom. Mel could sleep in the back, but you had to walk through Van's bedroom to get to the kitchen, bathroom and second bedroom—no privacy allowed. Mel wasn't fully happy with the arrangement, especially as Joanie virtually moved in and then Van's crazy brother and sister-in-law came to town from Seattle to enjoy the opera season and wine-tasting which they did day and night as they argued over operas and wines night and day.

Mel was lonely and miserable, his only campus friends, Norman Meineke and Leonard Gardner off in their own worlds as soon as classes let out each day. As politics heated up in Berkeley, the most San Francisco State could muster at first was a campaign among the literati signaled by their motto, plastered all over campus: *Stamp out Henry James*. Meanwhile Gardner worked on another draft of what was to become *Fat City*. And Meineke kept writing away at one story after another without, it seemed, ever having any success. Both of them lived in couple arrangements, and Mel realized he was virtually the only one he knew who was totally alone.

Soon Joanie became pregnant, and it became clear to him that he had to leave the happy couple behind and find his own way as soon as possible. So he raced all over town looking for a new place, finding one on Division Street just a few blocks above the Filmore area and on the edge of Pacific Heights. It was another studio cheapo, smaller perhaps than the Sunset apartment, but with its own entrance onto the street. It was from here that Mel struggled with his writing, drafting "The Little Boy Who Flew Away," a story with excruciating detail about being fat, bullied and isolated, losing all hope of love or health; and he also drafted his dismal, lifeless play, *Still Another Barroom*—a tribute to *The Iceman Cometh* and *The Time of Your Life*, but also to Jean Genet's *Balcony*, drafted in his final undergraduate year.

It was from his new home that he cruised the area seeking women out of his loneliness and horniness, teaming up finally with one at a bar who invited him to her house, where they engaged in foreplay, until, her period gone berserk, she was bleeding all over the bedsheets and him, and screamed him out of the house.

One night, Van and Joanie invited him over to their new beach apartment to celebrate her imminent birthing, and he found himself flirting with Joanie's fiftyish mother as they walked on the beach and, separated from Van and Joanie, even kissing the woman in a crazy moment. He thought little of it all until Joanie gave birth and Mel came to visit her in the hospital, and ran into the mother, who eventually made her way toward the elevator, with him following her, waiting with her, and then entering and starting to kiss and touch until the elevator reached the ground floor. She had to leave for L.A., she said, her husband was waiting. But they made out in her car, and he finally brought her to orgasm. She kissed him and apologized for her lack of time to reciprocate, but promised to visit him soon, leaving him off at a train station as she buzzed her way onto the freeway for her drive to the airport. (Later she sent him a sweet letter, but he decided not to respond, never saw her again, and never felt comfortable with Joanie again).

It was only days afterward that he ran into Eileen Cotrell, the Italian-Irish student actress he'd met in Berkeley and who now became a key figure in his life during the first half of his senior year in college.

2. Italian Days and Plays in the City

They met one day, at the side entrance of the Humanities Building on the San Francisco State College campus as he heard a voice behind him that had some kind of familiar ring and then turned around to see, oh so close to him, Eileen.

"Hello," he said.

"Hi," she responded, though with a tentative register. "Don't you remember me?" he said. "At the Dwinelle little theater, when you played Jocasta, Amanda and Laura, and then we met at Robbie's when I told you you were great and you said someday I'd have to tell you more about it..."

"Of course, " she said. "Now I remember—and what more do you have to say about it?" She laughed, and then, apparently feeling she'd put him too much on the spot, she put her hand on his forearm, and said. "Sorry, really you don't have to answer that... But tell me how you got here to this unimpressive functionalist campus and this supreme example of urbanist vulgarity that dares bear the name of Humanity!"

They both laughed at her histrionics, and then he answered her most prosaically, "I had troubles in Berkeley and I couldn't stay,

so I came to the city and here I'm finishing up my B.A. And you?"
he quickly added.

"Well, I graduated in theater and tried to get some acting gigs
but nothing seemed to work out, so I decided to come back to my
mom's house in the Sunset District and get a teaching credential
here."

Mel felt crestfallen. At first her magic was as before, but
hearing her story, the aura began to dip. "I'm sorry to hear that,
because you really are great, and you shouldn't give up. There's
plays opening all over this little town and maybe you can still get it
going."

"Well, yes," she said, "but somehow it's not all so important
as it might have seemed in Berkeley when we were all wrapped up
in theater."

He tried to convince her otherwise, telling her about his feeble
playwriting efforts and the drama courses he was taking. He invited
her to a coffee and talked about the brazen director, the famous and
student plays they'd worked on and everything they could think of.
Despite the lost aura, or perhaps because of the loss, he found it fine
being with her.

She was not a great beauty, something which he had already
known even when he was first smitten with her. She was too short
for that, and while she was hardly fat, she seemed somehow too
ample for her frame and a bit flat chested, he estimated. But this did
nothing to discourage him—not even her fall from the illusions of
great grace. She was after all more reachable, a normal woman
hopefully looking for a normal happy relation with a not so normal
but at least normal-seeming though desperately lonely young man,
a few years her junior and not sure if he had any future—in love
with theater and the idea of writing plays but not at all sure if the
life of someone in the theater was something for him.

They talked on and on and finally agreed to go to a play
together at the nearby Conservatory of Music. They dated more than
a few times, with long post-theater talks about the play, the

director—all of it. Perhaps, he felt, something was developing between them, though there was hardly a kiss, hardly anything physical between them at all. Their affair was going to the theater, seeing every local group and every visiting company arguing, about every play and presentation. Was that a proper treatment of Italian Americans in *View from the Bridge*? Wasn't *Death of a Salesman* a Yiddish Odets play in Anglo drag? But mainly they (or was it he?) always chose plays with big and beautiful parts for women: *Medea* and not *Oedipus* after all, *Macbeth* and not *Julius Caesar, Hedda Gabler* and not *The Master Builder, Miss Julie* and not *The Ghost Sonata.* And of course Tennessee Williams, all of Tennessee Williams, and their most recent favorite by Edward Albee, which Mel called *Who's Afraid of Eileen Cotrell*? Or *Who or What's Eileen Cotrell Afraid of?* That's at least what he told her, urging her to go for it, to start acting again, to try playing the part, to be Amanda or even Josefina or Blanche, but not Laura.

One day, they started listening to opera together and going when they could afford it; they bought records and fought for hours about who was better, Callas or Tebaldi, or about who was best for Bellini or Puccini, Donizetti or Verdi. Then they went to see all the Italian movies they could, by all the great directors, with Anna Magnani, Silvana Mangano, Gina Lollobrigida, Giulietta Masina, Monica Vitti, Sophia Loren and of course, with many if not all of them, Marcello Mastroianni. But really, their greater love was Italian theatre, as they went to *Enrico IV* and *Six Characters*, along with the early plays of Ugo Betti and Dario Fo. Most striking of all was Giorgio Strehler's Piccolo Teatro di Milano when they came to perform *The Servant of Two Masters* in a one-nighter at the Geary Theater (Mel wrote an essay about the performance as an example of Artaud in action).

They were given to summer walks through North Beach by the San Francisco church and the statue of San Francisco that Ferlinghetti had written about; they watched the old-timers playing bocce ball, browsed at the City Lights Bookstore, and then ate at one of the area's incredibly cheap and marvelous Italian eateries. Or they went over to Fisherman's Warf past Aliotto's, DiMaggio's, Scarappelli's and other Italian fish joints, until they reached the best viewing place on the dock to look out toward Alcatraz and imagine Capone's days on the Rock. Then, returning to their prime obsession on another day, they walked around Mel's neighborhood in lower Castro, near the Mission District, and found a little theatre Mel had heard about, walked in the door and found a group rehearsing Maxwell Anderson's *Winterset*. They watched the inept actors working through the text, trying their best to bring alive a play that was too overladen with weak verse and murky atmosphere to do justice to the Sacco-Vanzetti case it sought to evoke. Pretty soon the actors noticed them and asked if they were just bumming around or maybe really interested in working with the group. And before you knew it, they were doing the lighting and sound, helping with props and even promoting the play throughout the neighborhood. Soon the play opened and their names appeared on the playbill.

"We're part of the group," he told her even as the production got terrible reviews and failed to get an audience. "But now our apprenticeship's over and we'll have to do more. You're going to try out for a part in the next show and I'm going to show them one of my plays." She seemed to agree, though she expressed some concern about the teaching certificate tests that were coming up.

3. Theater Dreams, Life Realities and Sweet Sorrow

Mel dreamed his dream of an ideal community theater—one in which dramaturges, directors and players collaborated in writing scripts based on events taking place in the world and the neighborhood, a minimalist theater almost without props and with no proscenium but also not a circle but a space that could be reconfigured and lit in relation to the materials at hand with plays that evolved as events or ideas changed from day to day, always eliciting audience opinions to map out alternative directions to be tried in successive days. He read an article about a community suffering from water contamination, somewhat like in Ibsen's *Enemy of the People*; and in three days, he feverishly drafted a play script, set in the North Beach Italian community, showing it to Eileen and then, at her urging, taking it to the theater group.

The director took days to read the script, and returned it, saying, "Not bad, it's a pretty good concept, but the only way we could make it feel real would be to work in a lot of Bay Area Italians—and I don't think that would be too easy. But your concept, your idea of a theater, isn't bad."

Mel submitted the play to his dramatic writing professor, Jim Scheville, who thought it had promise. They even went so far as to meet with an Italian American club on campus to see if they would be interested in doing the play. But the students balked, said Mel was trying to make fun of their community, that the whole thing seemed more like the old radio show *Luigi* and it just wouldn't fly.

Then Mel decided to send the manuscript to his special playwriting friend, Jay; and sometime later he went to Berkeley with Eileen to see the campus production of Jay's first performed play, in that same little theatre where he'd first seen Eileen as Jocasta. The play was so well written, so powerful, that they were both stunned. They went with Jay and a few friends over to their old haunt at Robbie's and laughed about the old days. Jay had been out of touch with Mel for some time, writing his plays, practicing his bass and playing on Friday nights at LaValle's.

"Didn't know you guys got together," he said laughing. "Well, I'll be," he said, belying the great verbal gifts so evident in his writing.

Mel looked at Eileen and realized she was never going to be his love, realizing for the first time too that he might never be a playwright like his ever-so-committed, disciplined and gifted friend. "Your play was so intense and powerful," he told Jay. "It just knocked me over. And all the time I thought I was a stronger writer than you and I see now it's not so."

"Well I work at it, it doesn't come easy," Jay gibed. "And it's not the kind of play I really want to write, but something I lived through and had to get out."

"Did you get a chance to read my play?" Mel asked him, with Eileen looking on.

"Yeah I did—" Jay said with something hollow in his voice.

"And what did you think?" he asked, sensing he already knew the answer.

"Well there's a lot of good stuff there, man, but there's a lot that just doesn't work and drifts away from the main point you're trying to make. Maybe you could work it up, but it might be better just to consider it an exercise and go on to something richer, maybe closer to your own world."

After a few beers, the couple excused themselves and drove back across the Bay Bridge to continue their San Francisco lives, both somehow knowing their dreams would never be. Eileen went on to take her certificate exam and then began searching for a job. Mel called to ask her out, to celebrate her achievement, but she instead invited him to a dinner she had long promised him she'd have her mother prepare.

Before dinner they drank wine and toasted Eileen's victory, her Sicilian mother so proud of her and so pleased that she drank more than was her norm. "To Eileen," she said. "Maybe she's more Irish like her dad, but she's my wonderful Sicilian-Irish daughter who's now going to be a professor!"

At that point Eileen let Mel know she had been hired as an English instructor at a community college south of the city. Mel was sad for her but pretended to be happy. "Yes," he said, "your daughter will be a wonderful teacher and I think she'll be able to pursue her acting too!"

"Well, maybe," said her mother, "who's to know—she's may be just a little too un-Italian for that."

"But the Irish have a great theatrical tradition, too," Mel objected, preparing to give a lecture about the Abbey theatre,

Synge, Shaw, O'Casey, Lady Hamilton, Yeats, Beckett and the whole caboodle.

"Yes," his mother acknowledged. "But it's fine to be a professor, no?"

"Being a professor's fine," he agreed, "but she has the gift."

"A gift you want her to share, but she may not be able to," she said.

Eileen just looked away while her mother went to the kitchen and came out with the most wonderful eggplant parmigiana of Mel's wildest Italian dreams. But even as he praised and savored the meal, he felt the saddest sense of longing and loss, which was perhaps even worse for its lack of intensity.

After dinner and the polite thank you's and ciaos, he and Ellen left the house and went for a walk on the beach. It was cold and foggy as usual but worth the walk in any event.

"My mother's always wanted the best for me," she said. "And she tried to encourage that spark she saw just as much as you. But when she came to see *Glass Menagerie*, she saw me come unraveled. I lost control of my parts—I just couldn't do them. I was paralyzed between Amanda and Laura and I just couldn't go on."

"Well that happens to all of us," he continued, "But life's an adventure. We can't be afraid to live it, we can't let someone stop us."

But she put her fingers softly but insistently on his lips, stopping his great speech. "I know it's not what you hoped for," she said, "but it's the way it is. I don't have the stomach for the theater, and I don't think you do either, to be honest."

"Why do you think nothing happened between us?" he said, defeated and knowing it.

"But a lot happened, we learned so much, enjoyed so much together."

"You know what I mean. Do you think something might've happened if I'd been more aggressive?"

"We would've ended sooner, is all, and you knew it really, which is why you didn't try."

"I was waiting for the right moment, which never came," he said mournfully.

"It just wasn't in the cards. You're a sweet man, but you're not my gentleman caller."

"Maybe if you'd been more determined to make it as an actress..." he suggested.

"You only responded to my Italian, theatrical side and not the rest of me. And you idealize the Italians— Mussolini and the mafia don't come from nowhere. And you're the one who just lectured my mom on the great Irish theater tradition."

He had to acknowledge she was right and admit he really knew nothing about the Italians, the Irish or practically anyone or anything.

"I think all this comes from you running away from being Jewish. I'll bet I'm the first non-Jew you dated for any length of time. And I'll bet you've never written a play about Jewish things."

Again he had to agree. "I guess I'm just too young and romantic," he added.

"And I'm too old and unromantic— not that I'm old enough to be your mother," she laughed.

"You can play both girlfriend and mother in any play of mine," he told her.

And they embraced as the wind and waves noised about them, and then they said goodbye.

Part VI. On the Road Too
(Spring Break 1961)

1. Linda from Berkeley to North Beach and Back

Bob told him she was all torn up, but he didn't really explain why. Just before they were supposed to go south, he played with Mel's mind, sensing his lonely friend was taken by this stewardess friend of Kara, Linda, and then telling him how she was totally lost because her best stewardess friend had died in a crash.

"Let's go over to see her where she's staying with Kara," he told Mel. "Let's see if you grab the moment or start to forget her before anything crazy happens."

They waited in the living room until she came out, smiled ever so slightly and then sank into a chair hardly talking as Kara chattered on and Mel didn't know what to say.

In a flash, Bob spoke up, saying, "Come on, let's go cross the bay for a drink or two."

Kara begged off, waiting for to come home and having to deal with her baby. "But you go ahead," she urged Linda. "You haven't been out for days."

Not his kind of woman, Mel supposed—blue-eyed Anglo or Irish, but some Native American strain that made her maybe interesting. Otherwise, she looked like a lot of the girls who wore short plaid skirts and let their knees and under-legs hang out almost reaching your leg while you sat in class marveling at the old man on the heath, or J. A. letting us go then you and I...

But the loss of her friend gave her a kind of tragic aura he couldn't resist. Attracted, he was now drawn to her, but Bob did most of the talking, taking the lead, supposedly for his friend.

"How are you doing, kid?" Bob asked her just as they got in the car.

And with that she started crying right off, leaning against Bob as the tears welled up. "It's hard," she said. "It was just like that."

Mel began feeling like the third wheel, when he was really the fourth—an idiot sitting in the back seat, falling in love almost right then and there, wanting to console her as Bob was doing, feeling out-ranked and out-flanked by this supposed friend of his—*Bob*, and knowing how later Bob'd say it was all for Mel. But was it really? Hard to know.

They crossed Berkeley and the Bay Bridge and pretty soon they were parked in North Beach and headed over to the Wine Cellar. They started downing beer-whiskey combinations and pretty soon got pretty juiced up, all three of them talking and not talking, joking and laughing or crying or whatever, until Linda got up clearly sick and needing to puke, which he guessed she did, though, tempted as he was, he didn't follow her to the bathroom. She took a long time and when she came out, she was somehow more drunk and sober at the same time.

"I'm slated to fly tomorrow," she said. "They gave me some time off when they gave me the news, but now they say I should come back, and I don't see why—I don't feel like flying anymore."

"Hey," Bob said, "Don't let 'em push you around, tell 'em you need more time."

"They'll let me go and just asking for time will clue them about me and tell them maybe it's better if I don't fly with them any more..."

"Well screw them," Mel said, wanting to get in the game. Linda looked up at him for a second, but it was like she was seeing a bug—or that's how he felt it.

And again she leaned on his supposed friend, crying into his shoulder, and whimpering some words Mel could hardly hear over the bar noise, something like "Those bastards, they've pretty much made their minds up about this any way. And I don't want to fly with them, I guess I'd rather give it all up—everything," she added. "I just want to call it all off."

Then Bob stopped trying to console her. He got up and say, "Let's get out of here," and in a flash, they were walking down the street past this bar and that and coming at last to a big pawnshop. In they went and Bob went right to the gun counter and asked to see some revolvers.

"What do you want with them?" I asked.

"Maybe I want to buy one and give it to Linda," he said. And suddenly she smiled and even gave him a little kiss. Bob began looking over one gun after another, and now she was looking too and Mel was even joking with her about the guns; and she finally looked at Mel again maybe out of charity, making a gesture to get him in on the big joke, even though he hadn't the faintest idea of what was going on.

"These are the best two," Bob said. "But this one's kind of big and maybe too hard to handle—while this one seems like it was made for a lady."

"Let me try it," she said, happier now than at any previous moment, even giggling for a second, at least so it seemed to Mel, while she played Bat Masterson with the lady gun, putting it in her hand, massaging it, aiming and even cocking it.

"Should we get it?" Bob asked.

"Yes," she murmured.

"You want some bullets?" asked the salesman, wishing to up his sale.

"No bullets, right," Bob insisted.

"O.k., o.k.—no bullets. I mean I can always get them later if I really want them, right?"

"Right," he replied.

"Yeah," I said, trying to join the game, and maybe even starting to understand what was going on.

"That's right little lady," chimed in the salesman now way off base, "we always got 'em in stock when you want 'em."

And all three of them rifled their pockets till they came up with enough cash. The gun number was taken. Linda showed her i.d. and the deal seemed cooked, when Bob took the gun, handed it to the salesman, and said, "On second thought, we should get the gun when we get the bullets."

The salesman shrugged his shoulder, apparently pissed, but trying to show he didn't give a damn. He put the gun away. Outside, she hugged them both, and kind of laughed. "You guys are great," she says, "but I have to get home."

So off they went, crossing the bridge again and delivering Linda to Kara, still unsure if she was going to get ready to fly or trip back across the bridge to get her gun and ammunition. "Thanks, guys, maybe you saved my life tonight."

Then Bob told her that he and Mel were leaving right away to L.A. but that they'd keep in touch and look her up when they came back. And of course, Mel knew they were going the next day, but all at once Bob said it's time to go, so they went home and packed; and probably before Linda's head could hit her pillow, they were cruising out of town already exhausted but set on driving south through the night.

Suddenly Mel told Bob he was crazy about Linda and felt lousy about leaving especially after he'd put a gun in her hand.

"Hey," Bob said, "That was the only way to stop her from getting one and using it."

"I hope you're right," Mel answered. "But it was kind of crazy."

"And don't you think you're acting crazy?" Bob asked. "Falling in love with a girl who's turned suicidal because her best friend's been killed. And you worrying she might want to be with me instead of you, when she can give a shit about either of us."

"What are you saying?"

"You figure it out," Bob answered as they went down the road.

2. Pete on the California Road

Mel fell asleep a few hours while Bob went racing along, passing one town, and heading toward another and beyond. He woke up in one god-forsaken hole when Bob filled the tank and then stepped into the truck stop café, them both plopping down at the counter asking for some pie and coffee.

"Hey," said a funny looking guy sitting next to Bob. "Where you guys coming from?"

"The Bay Area," Bob said.

"You don't say," he said. "You wouldn't be heading toward L.A., would you?"

"Yeah," Bob answered, "Van Nuys for him and Long Beach for me."

"Well, he said, "I don't wanna be too forward, but could you guys give me a lift to L.A.?"

Bob looked him over and Mel did too. The guy looked too weird to him, with bug eyes staring out of rimless glasses—something a little wild in his gaze, a backpack on and big boots, faded plaid shirt and a crazy green hunting cap on his head.

"Sorry," Mel was about to say.

But then he heard Bob say, "Sure, why not? Maybe you'll keep my co-pilot awake."

So sure enough it was three of them flying down the road like Kerouac characters heading south including one guy who looked to be flipped out and crazy.

"Yes sir," he started, as if someone had asked him. "I been going up and down this road since I got out of the army. See, I got out and went looking for my wife, but when I got home, I found her shacking up with some guy and so then I cornered them and knocked the shit out of both of them, and went off to cool off and when I got back they were gone, though I found out he went one way and she went another. And I've been looking for her up and down this road ever since."

"Maybe she doesn't want to be with you now that you've gone and beat her and her friend up," Bob suggested ever so sweetly.

"Well now I understand that sir—what's your name?"

"Bob. What's yours?"

"Let's just say they call me Pete."

"Okay, Pete, I'm sure you can't be beat," Bob offered.

"No sir, Bob, you're right there, but you kind of got me wrong. You see, this girl, my wife, she is a bit of a slut, but really, she's sweet and I know she loves me. She really loves me, but she gets real lonely and antsy when she's alone too long, and I kind a left her alone when I was over there, drinking and whoring my way through one town after another. So even though she did me wrong and deserved to get hit and more— maybe much more—I know she really loves me and once she gets over being scared of me, she'll want to be with me all over again."

"Wouldn't be so sure about that, after that beating you gave her."

"No," Pete insisted. "You don't understand, women they can't help themselves—they need lots of loving. And if you're not there they can't help themselves, so it's the husband's job to keep his wife in line. And If she runs, and of course she's gonna run, it's his job to find her and bring her back."

"I don't know about that, Pete," Bob said, and now Mel knew his friend was crazy because he was egging on a crazy man who already owned up to having a pretty violent side.

"Seems to me you're really looking for her to give her what you think she's got coming, that you're still pissed as hell and if you find her, you're going to bash her head in or something..."

"No!" Pete protested, and he even took off his glasses, so Mel could see his buggy-buggy eyes in the mirror. "You got it wrong," Pete continued. "I love her, she's my woman, I want to find her and be with her the rest of my life. I'm gonna look for her up and down these California roads till I find her. And when I find her it's gonna be great, it's gonna be something wonderful—"

"Come on, Pete," Bob taunted him, egging him on even more. "Stop fooling yourself. You're never gonna find her and if you do, you're gonna kiss her but right in the middle of that kiss, you're gonna get all upset, cause you know she's a whore and she's giving blow jobs to every prick that passes close by..."

"No," Pete moaned.

"Yeah, Pete you better face it, you've got something deep dark in you ... look in the mirror," Bob said, opening up the visor mirror right in front of Pete. "There you are my friend; there's you and you've got murder in your big buggy eyes."

Then Pete looked and looked again and started to cry. "No, no," he whimpered. Then he said, "Pull over, stop the car." And Bob pulled over and stopped the car. "You got it all wrong, you," Pete said, yanking the door open and getting out. "You're just spreading shit on me and my wife. And you're wrong. I love her, I'll never hurt her, and you can—just go and fuck yourself!"

And with that he slammed the door and walked off, crossing the highway as if he wanted to go back to where his wife might be or just where this terrible ride began. Meanwhile Bob stepped on the gas and took off.

"I guess he didn't want to go to L.A. as much as he thought he did," Bob quipped.

3. Tripping from L.A. to San Luis Río Colorado

Bob dropped Mel off in Van Nuys, and Mel stayed with his parents, eating Jewish soul food, thinking about Linda and Pete, but also eager to hear from his friend to see if they were going to take that trip south of the border they'd been talking about forever. And sure enough,

Bob finally called him and said, "Look, take the bus down to Long Beach and we'll spend a day or two in Mexico."

So it was goodbye folks, and off Mel went on the Greyhound, his luggage on his back, waiting at the station no more than a few minutes until Bob drove up and with a yelp or two, they were off to the border. Somehow it seemed endless getting to San Diego and then San Ysidro; and then, for the first time in his life, Mel crossed a border into another country—that country that would be the land of his dreams for years to come.

He couldn't believe it when the border guards just waved them on, when they got 24-hour car insurance for some five bucks.

Suddenly, they were on a dusty street that was supposed to be the main drag but had nothing too much going on except some tourist stores and restaurants and some crazy bars that hadn't opened yet and a zebra-painted donkey that dropped his shit in the street in the early afternoon. They drove around not finding any place they wanted to stop.

"This place is just the border's worst hellhole," Bob said, "Let's see something else."

They came to a sign showing Ensenada south and Tecate east, and Bob choose the eastern route taking them to the dusty brewery town that was just too small and dead for them to stay. So they drove on what turned out to be a mad curving road, curving/curving past one insane rock formation after another, just missing a crash with a falling rock one minute and with a veering truck in the next. Somehow, they got to Mexicali and Mel had his first beer and tacos on the other side. But this town was the ugliest they had seen yet and Bob said, "let's get out of here too."

But then on the outskirts, they had to stop for gas and Bob started talking Spanish to a lady who also sold him some coffee and invited him to meet her daughter, who turned out lovely enough and immediately got Bob got into a card game. "The lady wants me to marry this sweetheart and save the family. But if I win, I don't have to marry her," said Bob. Somehow the daughter won and Bob said, "Well, we'll be back for the wedding in a few days."

At least that's what Mel thought he said, because he didn't understand a word. Bob even kissed the woman and her daughter, and told Mel to do the same, which Mel did, not knowing what he was doing nor why.

Off they went down another road but pretty straight this time, and Mel said, "I can't believe I'm so deep in another country."

And Bob laughed, "Deep, huh? We've been riding parallel to the border all this time—we're just a few football field lengths away from the border."

It was just some twenty miles more down the road where they got to San Luis Río Colorado, and Bob drove around the miserable little plaza, looking for god knew who or what.

"We need some marijuana," he told Mel.

"We do?" Mel asked.

"Sure, and more" Bob said, driving up to a guy with

sunglasses standing under a plaza arch, getting out and talking to the gentleman, then waiting as he went off and then, when he returned with some unidentifiable somethings (maybe a pouch, maybe a bottle—probably both), giving him some money for his trouble.

"Tequila and hash," Bob announced triumphantly as he hopped in the car and took off. The sun was starting to set, and he chose the old bullring on the outskirts of this small town as the place for sharing his treasures, both of which were pretty new to Mel.

"A virgin in everything," Bob laughed, and gave Mel a swig and a toke and on went their evening party.

"I'm in Mexico!" Mel screamed.

"Ha!" Bob said, happy to see Mel getting loose.

"In *Me-hico*," Mel said, trying to get it right, and he didn't know a word of Spanish.

"Look up," Bob told him, "And say, 'El cielo es azul.'"

Mel looked, and saw it was dark but somehow understood what Bob meant and he repeated, "El cielo es azul."

"And the moon," Bob continued, "La luna es de queso!" And so Mel came to say his first two sentences in Spanish of the many he would learn over the years. They were sitting in the car, contemplating the bullring, the sky, the moon, and finally Bob said, "Now man, the day's gotta be complete—we gotta get you laid— que viva Mexico!"

Mel knew it had to be at last, after all the failed and miserable efforts, the moaning over loves lost (but hardly had), the sad encounters and terrible defeats with this one and that. And so now he put up no resistance as Bob drove back to the plaza, and after a few questions in his Spanish, broken no doubt, but so infinitely better than Mel's, he found how to go to the nearest brothel.

There they parked and were ushered in. A band was playing and a plump none-too-attractive woman was gyrating on the stage. They paid little attention to the entertainment, but just ordered and downed their drinks. Soon the waiter was asking whether they'd mind if a few ladies joined them. Bob told him to go easy and let them know it was for no more than one drink.

"This is how they get your money," he said. The two women took their seats and started making a big fuss about how big they were.

"Big gringos," said one, eyeing Bob and the other said, "him big too!"

"Not so big," the other said, "But maybe big enough!"

She laughed, as did her friend—with Bob looking pretty amused and Mel just tense as the group's sax player led the other musicians in clunking out the sounds for one not so hot dancer after another. Then came the drinks and then another round. Bob had told him to be careful, but he also told Mel to go for it when his probing hooker friend started urging him to spend some private time with her.

"Come on honey, I no bite. Lisa give you a real good time, you won't regret it."

The more Mel drank, the better looking Lisa got and before he knew it, he'd agreed to a figure that Bob had really arranged, and he went off with his true love to their honeymoon suite, while Bob sat there, now smoking a cigar which came from where Mel just didn't know or care, Bob waving him on, as he just leaned back and seemed to enjoy the bar's happy cultural activities.

The suite was all in red and reeked with heavy perfume. He started trying to embrace his new love, but she backed off, saying, "No honey without the money, ok?"

At which point Mel paid his dues and she got sweeter, taking off her bra, letting him hold and suck on her breasts while she comforted his rod and his staff, until he was getting to fever pitch, with her now lying on her back and ready to receive what she probably hoped was a real quick quickie. But really just as Mel was ready to make her all her dreams come true, there was a knock on the door, and in came his favorite Mexican sax player, instrument in hand, urging her to pause in her social work to help him out.

Sure enough, she slid away, saying "wait a minute, honey," went to her friend, and then turned back to Mel and told him, "he need a fix."

And before he could say boo or discuss the evils of excess, his true love whipped out a syringe and an arm tube and began to inject him with the elixir of heroin he was so eager to savor. Mel was of course beyond speech, just watching, thinking about where he was and what he was observing, his sweet erection shriveling to nothing as he took in the scene.

"Feel so good," the sax guy managed to say, shaking his head, squinting and smiling clearly savoring an intense pleasure. "Wanna try it?" he offered.

"No thanks," Mel managed to answer.

"Bueno, nos vemos," said the Mexican Bird, a real gentleman and music artist, as he left the room.

"Okay, honey, I'm all yours again," said his true love.

"Thanks," he replied; but he knew it was pretty hopeless now and after some futile tries, he got up and said he was sorry.

"Me too," she said. Maybe you get it up some other time."

"Yeah," Mel said, wondering if it would ever happen. When he caught up with Bob, his friend was still smoking the cigar, but holding on to two hot ladies.

"Ready to go?" Bob asked, and when Mel nodded yes, he just slid out from under the ladies, mumbled something like gracias, threw down some cash and walked with Mel out of the club.

"All went ok, right?" Bob asked when they got to the car.

"Yeah sure," Mel said, but didn't tell Bob what had happened; and soon they were in the car and driving again.

4. Swimming in the Salton Sea

They didn't sleep and were driving now through the night, going back to Mexicali, crossing the border at Calexico and then driving north.

"Let's stop at the Salton Sea," Bob said. "I hear it's a beautiful place to rest."

They got to some likely spot just as the sun began to rise. They took out some blankets and lay down, looking up at a million stars. "El cielo es azul," Mel repeated, before falling asleep.

When they awoke, the sun was blasting away, and Mel lowered his gaze to see a beautiful blue sea, bluer than the sky on this cloudless morning.

"Let's go for it," Bob said; and with no one around, they got into the water with just their underwear. Soon they were floating on saltwater and just lazing about in a blue soup with a glaring sun. Mel finally told his friend what happened in the brothel, and Bob laughed some.

"Well, at least you've taken a big step," he said, probably not realizing how much of Mel's future life might be tied up with Mexico, Spanish and Latinas, how much has been laid out for him with Bob these last several hours.

Mel wondered if he would ever get it right, but the water made him feel so great, "I'm getting clean, purified, baptized, so I can start life again," he said. "Still," he told Bob just before they got out of the water, "I love Linda and want to be with her."

"After everything I've told you?"

"Maybe because," Mel said defiantly.

"Ha!" Bob exclaimed, "You're crazier than Pete."

"Why not?" Mel said as he and Bob started up the coast and they returned first to Long Beach, and then, a few days later, to the Bay area once again.

Part VII. Undergrad Road's End (Summer 1961)

1. Auto Procurement

Late spring came, and, very much alone, his B.A. in hand but broke and without any serious and sustained experience in love or life at the age of 22, Mel moved on to the job market to see what would befall him. No luck for days until a job hunter finally got him an offer he couldn't refuse, with an outfit called Auto Procurement Services.

This firm advertised in military newspapers the fact that those finishing their tours of duty or with extended breaks could order the car, year and model of their choice, and the company would seek it out, detail it and have it ready to go on their arrival in San Francisco. So G.I. Joe would order his car, and the job was to check out all the used cars available in the Bay area and beyond, find the closest they could to the car ordered and have it ready on arrival.

Of course it might be hard to find a green and white 1958 Pontiac convertible, in time, so for as low a price as possible the company would get a car close to the specifications (maybe a 1956 Ford sedan or a 54 Buick) and try to convince you to buy it at a price only a $500 to $1000 more than the requested high end limit. The client was under no obligation to take the car and was free to request something else or search for one of his own. But the usual case was that he had to get some place fast, or even worse, his family was there to meet him, so they could all drive back to Kentucky together.

Mel was impressed by the AP's noble effort to provide military men with the car of their dreams. But as his job developed, he began to see the dark cynical side of it all, as the staff rarely killed themselves in looking for the exact match car, but mainly dealt with one somewhat reliable dealer who supplied them with cheap cars somehow making vaguely plausible substitutes for the cars ordered. That some of these cars had been in terrible accidents and were doctored to look almost as good as new, that some of them might have engine or transmission problems that might emerge within days after purchase (but now miles away)—these were among the unpleasant aspects of AP's downside.

Mel's job was mainly picking up the chosen cars, trouble-shooting what had to be done to get the car ready for sale, and detailing the cars at the lowest price possible. Sometimes, too, he would pick up the customer at dockside or at the airport to bring him to the office, or set him up for the weekend hotel he'd ordered while he got ready to travel on Monday—all this, plus hosting the client, giving tips on places to eat, sites to take in, and even hooker services to ring up—anything could be part of the job.

In the course of all this, his job was to do all he could to create a deal-closing atmosphere for the client, to calm him when he realized that the car they had waiting for him had nothing to do with the car he'd ordered, to get him to see the charms of the car they were trying to dump on him, to get him to overlook the dents and dings that they simply couldn't deal with in the required time frame.

It was all too horrible for Mel and got worse day by day, week by week. After a month, he'd not sold a car himself, and he even had confidentially or indirectly convinced more than one soldier not to make the deal and end up with the real lemon he was being offered. Inevitably, one irate customer, violated Mel's confidence and actually quoted his words to his bosses. At which point, an obvious failure in this noble enterprise of helping our servicemen, Mel was called into the office of his supervisor.

"Mel, we're going to have to let you go."

"But why? I've risked my life trying to sell your lemons."

"That's the point, it's your goddamn negative attitude."

"Well you guys should stop conning service men."

At that Dick lifted his 250 pound frame from his chair and looked ready to beat Mel up. But then he paused, smiled and embraced Mel.

"Look kid, this just wasn't for you. It isn't easy to be so crooked and you just don't have it in you. I've no choice—I'm stuck with this job, but you're not. Good luck," he said, hugging him and then showing him out the door.

2. Son, Father, Past and Future

Mel decided that he could get by for the rest of the summer and that to get on with his life, he'd better register for the San Francisco State Creative Writing M.A. He then called his parents to tell them his plans and see whether they might be able to help him at all. Their finances had recovered somewhat after the failure of the coffee shop because his dad had latched onto some paid catering gigs at the Rodef Shalom Temple where they were members.

Now, as he told his father about his grad school decision, his father all but interrupted him with some important news. "Been meaning to call you, son, but you know we'd been volunteer caterers at the temple and lately they'd actually been paying us some for the jobs. And now we've just signed on to be their official permanent and paid caterers at the synagogue. So, we're on our feet at least for a while, and we'll be able to help you some, though, yes, you'll need to get a job as well."

What a sense of relief Mel felt, after so many woes and worries—so much *simus*, as he'd heard relatives say. "That's totally great," he answered. "I'm so glad. I know it's not what you dreamed of but it's something."

"Yes," his father said wearily, "It's not what I'd hoped for, but it's the best we could do and, yes, we'll survive."

"Great," Mel repeated. "But no, don't expect me to come to work for you at the Temple. I'm planning to look for a job as soon as I work out my grad school admission papers, so I'm going to be tied up working things out here."

In all of this, he heard the continued note of sadness from his father. "Make sure you're doing the right thing," he said. "Don't make mistakes like me."

"Don't worry, Dad." he assured him. "All the mistakes I make will be mine."

So now, relieved of many basic worries and doubts, his road to the future in process, what could be finer than his now liberated summer, especially since Jack had just come back from Paris and had left Mel his new Berkeley phone number and address. Soon he made his call to Jack, thrilled to hear his voice, and then made his way across the Bay Bridge to spend a few days with his friend—without knowing that with his dreams of Eileen and Linda all but behind him and even his love affair with Mexico already launched as a part of his developing life, and then with his parents and above all his errant father more or less ok, Mel's early California life was over and his new life was about ready to unfold.

About the Author

Marc Zimmerman is Professor Emeritus of Latin American and Latino Studies at the University of Illinois in Chicago (UIC) as well as World Cultures and Literatures and Hispanic Studies at the University of Houston, where he served as chair (2002-2008), involving considerable work with Latin American Studies programs. Zimmerman served in Nicaragua's Ministerio de Cultura during the first year of the Sandinista Revolution. He has been director of Global CASA/ LACASA Books since 1998; and he has written and edited over forty books on world, Latin American and Latino cultural and literary studies. He has won Fulbright, Rockefeller, Puerto Rican Studies, and other major awards; he has served on the jury of Cuba's Casa de la Américas, and been guest professor at McGill U., as wells as universities in Madrid, Puerto Rico, Nicaragua, and Tucumán, Argentina.

While Zimmerman holds a Ph.D. in Comparative Literature from the U. of California San Diego, he also holds an M.A. in Creative Writing from San Francisco State U., where he studied with Walter Van Tilburg Clark, Her Blau, Irving Halperin, Mark Harris, James Scheville, Ray West, and Herbert Wilner. His early stories were published in *The Dartmouth Quarterly*, *Descant*, *The Great River Review,* and (in translation) *Nuova Prosa*, a key fiction journal in Milan, Italy. More recent stories have appeared in the Chicago Latino online journal, *El BeiSMan*, as well as in *Voices in Italian Americana* and *Literal*, a Latin American literary journal.

In 2023, Zimmerman published his book on the rise of Chicago Mexican and Chicano writing; and he continues coordinating the development of a series of interviews and related materials entitled "The Chicago Latino Artist Series Project (CLASP)," which he donated to the Smithsonian American Art History Collection. Based on this ongoing work, Zimmerman has thus far published books and CDs centered on Chicago Mexican artists José Gamaliel González (2010 and 2013), Aaron Kerlow (2015) and José Guerrero (2016); he has presented and published work on Chicago Central American and Puerto Rican art, as he develops a book based on his Chicago Latino art research.

Returning to his first love of creative writing, Zimmerman has also been developing a book series of books of "autofiction" (related life-based stories, dreams and fantasies organized into novel-like structures), *Illusions of Memory* touching on Jewish, Italian, African and Central American, but above all Mexican/Chicano, Central American and Puerto Rican themes— with eleven books published and several others in progress, and with four volumes translated into Spanish and one into Italian.

In recent years, Zimmerman has lectured on Chicago Latino art at Dartmouth College, the U. of California Berkeley and San Diego, Purdue U., and the Universidad de Costa Rica. He has read from his fiction in Italy at Milano's Verso Bookstore and the Torino International Book Fair, in California at the University Press Book Store in Berkeley, the Tía Chucha Cultural Center and Pop-Hop Books in the L.A. area, the Media Center in San Diego, the Avid Reader in Davis, and the Green Arcade in San Francisco—as well as in public libraries in East Los Angeles and La Jolla. In Chicago, he has read for the Palabra Pura program of the Guild Complex, the Heirloom Bookstore, the Lozano Public Library, 18th Street Casa Cultural and Pilsen Community Books. In Puerto Rico, he has read at Librería Laberinto in San Juan and Librería Candil in Ponce, as well as in a seminar at El Centro de Estudios Avanzados in El Viejo San Juan. For additional presentations, he may be reached at tel. (281) 513-9475 or mzimmerman1939@gmail.com. To visit his author's website and above all his Illusions of Memory series, visit www.marczimmerman.net.

He and his wife Esther Soler from Quebradillas, Puerto Rico, divide each year between the island and the Wicker Park/ Humboldt Park area of Chicago. They continue to travel each year to Minnesota and California—to Mexico, Europe, and wherever else they can.

Marc Zimmerman's Illusions of Memory Series
(to order books, visit www.lacasachicagobooks.org)

Cycle I. Narratives organized by theme, ethnicity, etc. cutting across various time periods:

The Short of it All (1940s-2017)

Spanish language edition: *Cuán alta la luna*

Stores of Winter (1940s-1960s)

The Italian Daze (1950s-2018)

Italian version: *La penisola non trovata I giorni italiani di un viandante perduto.*

Lines on the Border (1961-1972)

Spanish language Selection: Amores Fronterizos

La Dolce Vita on the Northern Side (1966-1972)

Sandino on the Border (1969-1981)

Spanish language edition: Sandino en la frontera

A Mexican Maze Without Borders (1967-2022)

Martín and Marvin 1982-2010)

Spanish language edition: Martín y Marvin,

Forthcoming Volumes on:

My Own Years

The Afro-Americans

Jewish Americans

Puerto Ricans

Central and South Americans

Cycle II: 1939-1981 (Complete)

Genesis (1939-1958)

West (1958-1961)

No Light from Heaven (1961-1966)

Black, Brown, and White on the Border (1966-1970)

Managua, Mon Amour (Nevermore) (1969-1981)

Cycle III: 1981 - ?? (forthcoming)

The In-Between Years (1980-1988) 2024

The Solid Years. Chicago, Puerto Rico, Guatemala World *(1988-2001) 2025*

Houston, Puerto Rico and the World (2001-2011) 2026

The Not So Golden Years. Chicago, Puerto Rico *(2011-?) 2027*